WHO AM I

A Little Book of Hope

JOE MILLER

Marco Productions

First edition

Editing, book design, and book cover by Caitlin Freeman
getbookified.com

Published by Marco Productions

ISBN: 978-1-7773910-0-3

To Mahmood Sarfraz
Thank you for your support
for my story a journey.
Best wishes and Good Health in 2022

DEDICATION

I dedicate this book to my wife Beryl, my son Mark, my daughter Tanya, and my grandchildren, Joey, Jordon, Justin, and Aysia. You are my family and my most treasured creation.

TABLE OF CONTENTS

PREFACE

After I came to, I lay there for what felt like hours. My skin was a mass of welts and bruises. At last, I forced myself to my feet, and I staggered off to find some meagre shelter for the night. It was then that I resolved to escape as soon as my body had healed sufficiently to run. For months now, I had played with the other children living on the streets, so I knew that it was possible to survive. I had watched as these children grabbed food for themselves when the vendors weren't looking, and I had seen the way they found little places to hide away from prying eyes at night. I didn't know if I could stay alive out there, but I knew that staying here meant a life of bondage, which to me felt worse than death. I don't know exactly what gave me the bravery to run. To think, I was just a little boy of six or seven. It took a few days to recover my strength. Then I plucked up my courage, and I ran away into the night…

This book is an account of my true-life story. As a child, I was one of thousands of orphans living on the streets of India during World War II. My early years were spent on the run. Many times, I was beaten, starved, and treated worse than a dog. I fled over 2,000 kilometres, from Jamshedpur in the north to Bangalore in the south, to escape a life of slavery.

All that I know about my early life comes from a handful of letters that were written about me while I was still a child. I have read these letters many times over, but they still offer only a few tantalizing clues to my origins. I have written this memoir to try and answer the question of who I am.

Mine is a story of hope and perseverance despite incredible odds. I have learned through immense struggle and misfortune that no matter how many times you fall, you must pick yourself up, dust yourself off, and continue on your journey. Never give up. Let adversity strengthen your resolve. I invite you to come with me on this adventure. I have faith that it will encourage you to keep moving forward in your life, wherever your path may lead you.

All my best to you.

— Joe Miller

WHO AM I

CHAPTER 1

To the best of my knowledge, I don't really know who I am. My origins are a mystery. I never knew my mother or my father, for I was given away shortly after I was born. What I do know is that my mother was Bengali, my father was European, and my birth in East India was most likely the result of a love affair during the years leading up to World War II.

My earliest memories are of St. Joseph's Convent Orphanage in Chandannagar, India (a suburb of Calcutta) and the Sisters who cared for me there. My mother, it seems, had died shortly after I was born, and I was entrusted to the care of a family friend. Even if she hadn't died, her family would have pressured her to give me away. A high caste Indian woman like my mother would have been shunned had she decided to keep an illegitimate child of mixed heritage. My mother's friend kept me for a few years. She must have fed me well and saw to my care, for I was a healthy and active child. Perhaps she even tried to be my surrogate mother, until she realized that she couldn't afford another mouth to feed. What I imagine is that this woman had children of her own, and as I grew, there was not enough food to go around. The bonds of friendship are often tested when resources are scarce, and whatever loyalty this woman may have felt toward my mother was overcome by the needs of her own family.

I was either two or three years old on 15th August 1935 when I was brought to the convent orphanage led by Mother Superior Marie Agnes. I suppose I was born around 1932, although I have no way of knowing my exact birthday. I was baptized on 20th August 1935, and I was given the Christian name "Joseph" by the Sisters in honour of their convent's patron saint. There is no record of what my original name might have been, or whether I had been given a Bengali or European name by my mother.

Years later in 1945, after I met the man who would save me from certain death, Mother Superior Marie Agnes wrote letters about what she knew of my birth and my early years. She explained that due to the convent's policies, she could make no enquiries about my parentage. In these documents, she stated that my Bengali birth mother had died, although she did not say how. What had ended my mother's life? Did she die in childbirth, or perhaps from disease? Or was she still alive, and feigning death as if to say, "don't come find me"? My father was stated to be English or Scottish, and this is borne out by a DNA test; however, no close relatives show up in my results for me to enquire about my family tree.

St. Joseph's Convent in Chandannagar, India.

These letters from the Mother Superior are some of the only scraps that tie me to who I am and where I come from. They are like tantalizing fragments from a puzzle that is missing the most important pieces. (See the original letters on page 172. The transcripts are on pages 44-45.)

St. Joseph's Convent was a kind of foster home for boys and girls who had no family. Some of us had lost our parents to accidents or disease. Some had been quietly dropped off at the orphanage because we were illegitimate or because our parents were no longer able to care for us. Others had gotten lost and were found wandering by concerned strangers who brought us to live with the Sisters. Whatever our origins, the Sisters allowed us to escape a life of begging or worse. When I think of it, I was lucky that my mother's friend brought me to St. Joseph's instead of simply casting me out to fend for myself. As I soon came to learn, there were thousands of children living their brief lives on the squalid streets of India, many of whom were little more than toddlers.

The Sisters of St. Joseph's Convent, Chandannagar, India.

The Sisters were kind to us. They ensured that we were fed, clothed, and as well cared for as we could be, given that we were all little orphans. The Mother Superior wrote that I had to be watched constantly, as I was always running about. She expressed concerns that

I seemed out of place with the other children, although this doesn't line up with my recollections. I don't remember anything particularly bad from that time. I recall mostly fun and happy things, like playing with the other orphans and looking for ways to amuse myself. Perhaps I pined for my mother's friend who had fostered me; however, I have no memories of missing her. The first motherly figures I recall in my young life were the strict yet caring Sisters.

I don't think I received any schooling at the orphanage. At least, I don't remember books or anything to do with lessons. That may have been due to my young age, for the convent did provide the older children with a basic education. Incredibly, St. Joseph's Convent still exists. It is now an all-girls Catholic boarding school in Chandannagar.

It seemed like life was pretty good for me at St. Joseph's, until the witch came along. The convent's mission was to rear and educate orphaned children and then place them in suitable homes. I do believe that the Sisters loved us and wanted us to be with adoptive parents who would care for us as their own. Perhaps in their haste to provide beds and food to the steady stream of new orphans who came to their doors, they did not adequately examine the motives of the families who came to pluck us from the relative safety of the convent. I had been at St. Joseph's for nearly three years, when on 12th June 1938, a woman named Mrs. Miller came to the orphanage to collect me. The Mother Superior described Mrs. Miller as an "Anglo-Indian lady from Tatanagar" (Jamshedpur), a city in East India nearly 300 kilometres west of St. Joseph's. Mrs. Miller had come to the convent to enquire about adopting a child, and she had apparently taken a "great fancy" to me when she saw me, perhaps because of my similarly mixed heritage. I knew nothing of this at the time. I was simply taken aside and informed that I would be leaving with her that day to live with her family.

A family scene in Jamshedpur, Jharkhand, India. 1957. It is possible that Mrs. Miller's family resembled the homey scene in this photograph.

I was eager to be part of a family, of course. All of us in the convent knew that it was better to be adopted than to remain an orphan forever.

However, Mrs. Miller frightened me, and I was sad to leave the Sisters who had been so kind. I had also heard rumors of bad things happening to little orphans like myself outside the safe walls of St. Joseph's, and I was scared of a terrible fate befalling me, as well. Ultimately, I had no choice in the matter. Mrs. Miller had picked me out of all the children in the orphanage, and so I now belonged to her. I was packed up and sent on my way, and I never saw the Sisters or Mother Superior Marie Agnes again.

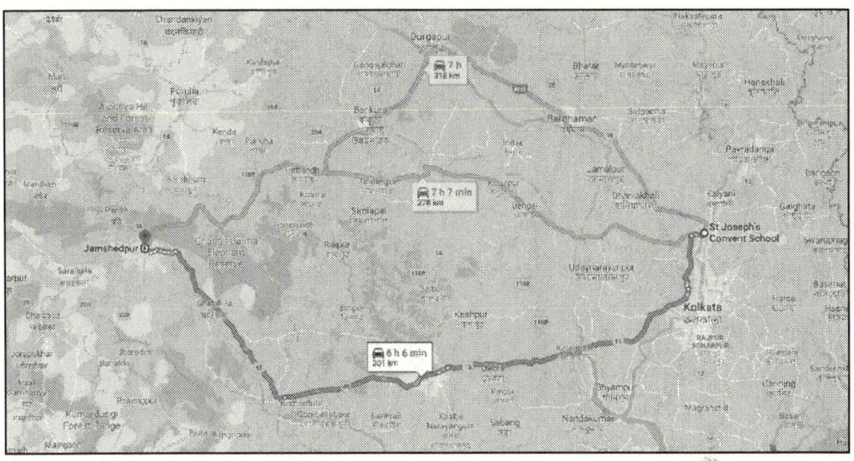

These are some possible routes that Mrs. Miller and I may have taken on my journey from St. Joseph's Convent in Chandannagar to her house in Jamshedpur.

I cannot remember the journey. My mind is blank. I don't recall any details of our route or our mode of transportation. I have tried to reconstruct the way that we may have travelled from Chandannagar to Jamshedpur. Looking on a map, there are several different itineraries that one can take today, but the route may have been different back then. Perhaps we took the 300-kilometre journey by automobile, or perhaps we travelled by train. Either way, what a long and harrowing passage that must have been. I think I must have blocked out those hours of my life. I wanted to forget them altogether. I had hoped that going to my new home would be a happy occasion, but it turned out to be worse than I could have ever imagined.

I still remember the feeling of shock and betrayal when I arrived at Mrs. Miller's house, and I realized that she had no intention for me to be her son. She already had children of her own. I was to be her slave. I had been taken away from the loving warmth of the convent, and now I was little more than somebody's dog. I don't remember ever interacting with Mrs. Miller's husband or her children. I wasn't even allowed to enter her house. I was kept outside, and I had to take shelter where I could find it.

Mrs. Miller made it clear to me what I must do if I wished to survive. I was to be her servant boy, and it was my lot to do tasks and run errands outside the house. If I did not perform to her satisfaction, she would beat me until I was bloody. I began by doing menial tasks round the grounds. Once I had proved myself trustworthy, Mrs. Miller would let me go out to complete small errands like buying goods for her at the local bazaar. It was there that I met other children my age who were out and about in the streets. Some of them were homeless, others were servants like me, and some lived in close quarters with extended families. As I played with these children, I learned what life was like on the street, and I began to figure out what a child must do to survive by himself. I didn't realize it at the time, but part of me had already started planning my escape.

The main street, Chaibasa, Jharkhand, India, circa 1910. I was used to seeing scenes like these on the streets of Jamshedpur.

I wished that I could figure out a way to return to St. Joseph's Convent. I thought that maybe the Sisters would take me back if I told them how terribly Mrs. Miller was treating me. She had abused their trust. They wanted the children that they rescued to be placed in loving homes with parents who would care for them and raise them well. I knew that the convent was far away from the city where I now lived, since it had taken more than a day's travel to reach Mrs. Miller's house. I felt more trapped and terrified by the day.

Mrs. Miller would punish me for every little thing. Some evenings, I would return late from the bazaar. The children I met in the street were the only people who would play with me, and some days I would get so wrapped up in our games that I lost track of time.

A market stall in Calcutta. 1945. Little street children like these were my only playfellows when I was a boy.

Mrs. Miller made sure to greet me with several strong whacks when I returned to her home. Those were also the days when she saw to it that I received no food. I was constantly hungry. I was never allowed inside, not even during mealtimes, so I never ate with the family. I was fed outside like an animal. I remember when monsoon season came, I was soaked to the bone every day. There was no shelter I could find that provided adequate refuge from the wicked rains.

Even on days when she decided to feed me, Mrs. Miller gave me very little to eat. I remember scant meals of fruit, rice, curry, and chapatis, which is the most basic fare in India. It was never enough, and my stomach was always grumbling. I remember once I was so hungry that when I was done running errands, I spent the leftover coins in my pocket on some food from a street vendor. My belly was full, but the punishment I received for coming home without any spare change made me wish that I had decided to go to bed hungry. I was made to strip down and stand stock still for hours with my arms outstretched until my whole body was shaking and I was exhausted to the point of collapse.

This was not the worst punishment I received, however. One of the tasks that I hated the most was bathing Mrs. Miller's parrot. The bird was territorial and fiercely loyal to Mrs. Miller, and he bit and scratched anyone else who tried to handle him. I can still remember how he would snap at me through his cage. He would slip his beak through the bars and inflict deep cuts into my fingers and hands. Mrs. Miller had a well in the garden area, and it was my job to dip the parrot into the well to cool him off when the temperatures soared. I was to leave the bird in his cage and lower him to the surface of the water and then bring him up several minutes later. Unfortunately, one day I put the parrot down into the well too far. Then I got distracted by another task, and I forgot about him. When I pulled him back up, I saw immediately that something was wrong. The bird was wet and lying limp in its cage. I tried to revive him, but it was clear that he was dead. I was filled with dread for what Mrs. Miller would do when she found out that I had killed her prized parrot. I was right to be afraid, for Mrs. Miller beat me until I lay unconscious and bloody on the ground.

After I came to, I lay there for what felt like hours. My skin was a mass of welts and bruises. Dried blood had mingled with dirt to cover my body in a sticky crust. I tried to crawl to the well so I could wash my wounds, but I collapsed after only a few paces. Misery and despair gripped my heart as I contemplated spending my days as a servant to that witch. It was a wretched life that lay before me. At last, I forced myself to my feet, and I staggered off to find some meagre shelter for the night. It wasn't safe to lie here out in the open in case Mrs. Miller decided to come back and give me another lashing. It was then that I resolved to escape as soon as my body had healed sufficiently to run. For months now, I had played with the boys and girls living on the streets, so I knew that it was possible to survive. I had watched as these children grabbed food for themselves when the vendors weren't looking, and I had seen the way they found little places to hide away from prying eyes at night. I didn't know if I could stay alive out there, but I knew that staying with Mrs. Miller meant a life of bondage, which to me felt worse than death.

I don't know exactly what gave me the courage to run away. To think, I was just a little boy of six or seven. However, the focused mind can accomplish astonishing things, and escape had become my single-minded obsession. It was the only thing that mattered anymore. It took a few days to recover my strength and gather the few provisions that I could safely stash for the start of my journey. I scrounged a bit of food and wrapped it up in a piece of cloth. I didn't have a bag, so I tied the cloth to the end of a stick and carried it over my shoulder. I found a place to conceal my meagre rations until I was ready to make my getaway. I had to keep the evidence of my impending escape carefully hidden from the Millers. One night, I waited until it was dark and everyone had gone to sleep. I gathered my food from the place where I had stashed it, and I listened for a while to make sure that none of the Millers were stirring. Then I plucked up my courage and fled into the night. I ran away from Mrs. Miller's estate as fast as I could, looking behind me all the while to make sure no one was coming after me.

CHAPTER 2

I ran as fast and far as my legs could carry me. I raced through the darkness along dirt roads, heading in the familiar direction of the bazaar. I ran toward the bustling city where the other homeless children made their homes. For I was now a homeless child, too. That realization hit me hard. I reached the city before the sun arose, and I found a little corner to hunker down for the rest of the night. I dared not sleep, for there were figures who prowled the streets, and I thought that some might be looking to capture unsuspecting children. The last thing I wanted was to be sold back into servitude. I huddled there, knees tucked up against my chest, shivering from fear and cold, and I tried to disappear into the shadows.

As dawn broke, the city began to awaken and bustle into the streets. My first order of business was to blend in with my surroundings. There were lots of other kids in the street, both boys and girls, so one more little boy was not going to make a difference. I know this in retrospect.

At the time, however, I was running in terror of Mrs. Miller. I was sure that she would send someone after me to grab me and drag me back to that horrible life of captivity.

A bazaar in Darjeeling, India, circa 1890. Bazaars like this were a common sight across India and were a good place to steal a few morsels of food.

I knew from watching the other children what I must do to stay alive. I must find sources of water, food, and shelter, and I couldn't delay. Without those vital resources, I would grow weak, and in my precarious position, death would follow soon after.

Luckily, I knew where to find sources of public drinking water throughout the city, such as water fountains with hand pumps. I knew about these fountains from my time serving Mrs. Miller. When the heat of the day got to be too much, I would crouch beneath them and pull the handle. It was a treat to feel the cool water flow over my body and soak my clothes. That was also how I showered. Many days it was so hot that by the time I got to the next pump, my clothes would be dry.

Two men taking their morning wash at a public handpump on the streets of Calcutta, circa 1950. I would seek out these handpumps in every city where I travelled.

I could never linger in one place for too long. Tarrying made me vulnerable to attack by anyone looking to take out their anger on a little child. Back then, the streets abounded with police officers hunting for pickpockets, shopkeepers protecting their wares, and other children defending their turf. Constant movement was the key to survival.

Food and shelter were the hardest essentials to obtain. Food could be stolen, of course, but if you got caught, the beating you would receive might cripple you, or worse. Shelter let you escape the elements and grab a few precious hours of slumber, since children weren't supposed to sleep outside. Railway stations were the best places to get some shuteye. There were so many travellers coming and going that few people would notice a little pile of rags sleeping in the corner. You had to keep one eye open, however, because the police could nab you if you lay down somewhere that was too conspicuous. I was in perpetual fear that the police would find me and drag me back to Mrs. Miller, and so I did everything I could to avoid them.

People waiting for their train at a Calcutta railway station. 1945. Railway stations like this were often good places to find shelter from the elements.

Whenever possible, I would beg or work odd jobs to earn some money. This allowed me to buy my food so that I wouldn't have to steal it from the street vendors. It was safer that way, and I was always one to avoid risk when I could. I learned my lesson the hard way when I was caught thieving one afternoon. I remember I had tried so hard to be careful that day. I glanced around to make sure no one was watching, and then I reached up to grab a piece of bread. I started moving away quietly to avoid attention, but at that very moment, the vendor turned his head and caught me red handed. He lunged at me, and I was momentarily stunned. I thought I had been so inconspicuous. He grabbed me by my tattered shirt and began to pummel and kick me so fiercely that all I could do was roll into a ball on the ground. I protected myself as best I could from his blows, but I truly did think that he was going to kill me. Eventually something must have distracted him. He stopped hitting me for a moment, and I took that opportunity to escape. I slithered out of his reach and crawled my way back into the anonymity of the crowd. I had to find a place to assess my injuries, and quickly too. If anything had been broken, my chances of survival would plummet. Luckily, everything seemed to be intact, just bloody and badly bruised. From that day on, I made sure that whenever I stole something, I would snatch it and dart away as fast as I could scurry.

I spent my days running, always running. I ran from city to city, never sure where I was going, just trying to stay one step ahead of death or capture. I kept one eye behind me at all times. No matter how far away I ran, I was terrified that Mrs. Miller might have sent someone to come after me. I had never interacted with her family or friends, since I had been kept outside, so I didn't know what any of them looked like up close. I was suspicious of every passerby who gave me a second glance and every pedestrian who happened to walk behind me for a little too long. Each was a potential associate of Mrs. Miller sent to grab me and drag me back to her. So, I ran from sunrise to sunset, each day feeling more like a hunted animal.

At this time, India was under British rule, and World War II had just begun, which meant that there were always British soldiers walking about. I needed money, and these white people seemed willing to part with their coins to employ industrious little Indian children.

A soldier reaching into his pocket to pay an Indian child for a shoeshine. 1945. I learned how to do odd jobs like this in my time living on the street.

Not long after I started to run, I watched as other boys would wait on railway station platforms and offer to carry the bags of weary Westerners who were all too happy to let a child tote their bag in exchange for a few rupees. I spent several days watching my fellow urchins prospect for work, and then I decided it was time for me to try my hand. It felt gratifying to earn a living, no matter how paltry it was. Of course, I would beg and steal whenever I needed to. Survival was my priority, and I wasn't above thieving to stay alive. But paying for food with money earned from work felt more secure than stealing from vendors or begging strangers for coins.

Children in a Calcutta railway station begging for coins and seeking out work. 1940. I learned how to earn money by observing street children like these.

I was still a small boy, no more than seven or eight years old, and I was very scrawny. I learned quickly that I could not haul suitcases with my bare hands for any length of time. I would squat down, hoist the suitcase onto my head, and balance it with my arms. Then I would scurry alongside the suitcase's owner as fast as my little legs would go.

When we got to the destination, I would set down the bag, hold out my hand, and watch as the traveller would reach into his pocket to place a few coins into my palm. When I look at how my life turned out, I realize that I have always sought out work for myself. I am always looking for the next job, the next opportunity, and I think I first learned that tenacious work ethic by trying to earn a meagre wage as a child in India.

As I pushed onward day after day, I began to grow bolder in my means of travel. In those days, trains lumbered slowly from city to city, at least compared to the trains of today. People who were poor or homeless couldn't afford a train ticket, so they would ride on top of the train. Hundreds at a time would climb onto the roof and hang on tight until they arrived at their destination. I remember when I first saw this phenomenon. I was slack jawed for a moment. How on earth did they get up there? Why didn't they come tumbling down? What were they holding onto? I soon understood that by cramming together like sardines, the crowds of people could stay put even when the train roared to life. I had never attempted to travel on the inside of a train. I didn't want to buy a ticket because I spent what little money I made on food. But I thought to myself that travelling on the top of a train could be a great way to put many more miles between myself and Mrs.

Miller. I could cover as much ground in one train ride as I could in a week of running.

Train surfers in Bangladesh. 2008. Nearly 80 years later, people in India still get around by riding on the top of trains.

The first time I travelled this way, I clambered up the side of the train when the guard wasn't looking and pulled myself onto the roof. The guards were ambivalent toward people who rode for free. They would mostly turn a blind eye, but I didn't want to give them reason to grab me and pull me down. If they called the police, the officers might figure out who I was and who I was running from, and then I would be done for.

When I reached the roof, I saw there were already dozens of other people sitting on top of the train car, and many more were climbing on behind me. There were little street children like me crammed next to men with tattered clothes and gaunt faces. We huddled together to keep from falling off the edge. We were a cross-section of India's poor. I did my best to be invisible as the sweeping glance of the guard passed over the train car where I crouched. The guard didn't spot me. After all, there was nothing that made me stand out. I was just one more little homeless Indian boy trying to eke out a meagre existence among thousands of other children just like me.

The rhythmic rattle of the train jostled my body. No matter how choppy the ride was, it was also comforting. Each clackety-clack took me further away from the horrible life I was fleeing. The more distance I put between myself and Mrs. Miller, the less likely she would be to find me. Some days, the roof was so packed that I would ride on the running board along the train's side. I would jump on when the train started pulling away from the station, and I would hang onto the door handle or anything else I could grab. When I was riding on the running board, I didn't have Mrs. Miller to worry about, but I still had to be careful of inspectors. The inspectors would wander through the train to make sure you had bought a ticket, and they could punish you if they caught you riding without paying a fare. Whenever I saw an inspector looking to make an example of someone, I would jump off onto the tracks and run. If the train were stopped or moving slowly, I would wait until the man had gone on his way. Then I would sprint alongside and scramble back onto the running board until the train reached its next destination. I would ride from city to city until exhaustion and hunger caught up with me. Then I would scamper down and search for food. Feeding my belly was always my main concern. I would buy a good meal whenever I had the money, but more often than not, my pockets were bare. Then I would steal a few morsels from a street vendor or scrounge for scraps in a rubbish bin. No matter how far I ran, hunger always caught up with me.

Cows lying on the sidewalk in Calcutta. 1903. Cows like these in various states of malnourishment were a common sight across India.

India is a vast country with a diverse landscape. As my winding route meandered its way from region to region, I remember the one constant was the cows. Hindus in India worship cows, and they believe that eating beef is sacrilege. They would rather see a cow become skin and bone than eat its meat, and yet they don't have the resources to care for the poor beasts. In every city along my travels, I would see starving and dead cows lying on the side of the road, covered in flies and dirt. It was a pitiful sight that reminded me of the fragility of my own life.

Luckily, I didn't see many dangerous animals on my journey. India has its share of deadly wildlife, from snakes to tigers, but I never crossed paths with these predators. If I had, I would be dead, especially if I had encountered any of the venomous snakes. In India, tens of thousands of people die each year from snake bites. I attribute my unlikely survival to my decision to stay within city limits and avoid venturing into the countryside. Cities had food, shelter, trains, and the safety of anonymity. Even though life in the city was dangerous, if I had tried to hide out in rural areas, I would have been more conspicuous and more at risk of attack.

I always travelled alone. During all the time I ran, I never had a single friend. I couldn't afford to get attached to anyone. It was a lonely existence. I recognized early on that if I associated with anybody, they could easily steal from me, attack me, or even kill me. There were some loose-knit gangs of street children who would work together to beg or pick pockets, but this never offered much protection. Someone could always stab you in the back if they saw you had something they wanted. No one made friends or had comrades—it just wasn't done. It was survival of the fittest. You couldn't think about anyone but yourself. We begged and robbed and did whatever we had to do to stay alive. It was worlds away from the loving shelter of the orphanage and the little boys and girls that I used to play with there. I have always been a bit of a loner, and I trace that tendency to this period of my life, surviving on my own as I trekked across the Indian subcontinent.

When I think back on this time, I wouldn't say that these were happy days, but they were days of freedom. I was free from the horrors of the life I would have led if I hadn't escaped from Mrs. Miller. I was free to do what I pleased, when I pleased, and I had no responsibilities other than staying alive. I was more like a little animal than a little boy. The memories of being loved by the Sisters in the orphanage grew fainter as my mind became fixated on the urgent and singular need to survive. As an adult, I shudder to think of how my life would have turned out if I had gone on living this way. There was no future, no past, and I was only concerned with the immediacy of the present moment. I lost all sense of the passage of time. I was living day to day, and I paid little notice as days turned into months and then years. Eventually five years passed by like sand slipping through my fingers. I spent the entire span of World War II running over 2,000 kilometres from Jamshedpur in the northeast to the city of Bangalore near India's southern tip. Of course, I paid little attention to the names of the places I passed through as I fled from one city to the next. I didn't have a destination. I just knew that I was running—always running.

Since it was the War years, there were many barracks with British soldiers stationed along my itinerant route. I learned from watching other children that I could stop into these encampments and get food from the officers. These soldiers were all too happy to share their provisions with grateful little orphans. It was a fair exchange. They would give us food, and we would give them a welcome respite from the horrors of war. I would play with the soldiers for an hour or two and then usually head on my way, running to catch the train into the next city. Then one day, out of the blue, I met a British serviceman who would change the entire course of my life.

CHAPTER 3

I will remember that day for as long as I live. It is one of my strongest memories from my nomadic childhood. It was January 1945, and after nearly six years on the run, my travels had brought me south to the city of Bangalore. Like always, I was in search of food. As the War raged on, it became easier to find army barracks in the cities where I sojourned, and they were a good place to get a tasty meal. The British soldiers in India were fed well—often better than their countrymen back home whose diet was limited by ration books—and they would give us better food than we could steal from the street vendors.

I was older now—probably on the cusp of thirteen—but I was small from malnutrition and looked more like a ten-year-old. I was an appealing child with an engaging smile and bright eyes, and I could speak some simple English, enough to gain the favour of weary soldiers who wanted a reminder of their children or younger siblings who were waiting for them a world away in England.

An RAF base in India during World War II.

That morning, I happened to be running toward a block of buildings that belonged to the Royal Air Force. Buildings like this meant people, and people could mean food. To get to the buildings, I had to run across a large rice field, which is a common sight in India. I ran through the tall grasses, which came up to my waist, my bare feet sloshing against the wet and muddy ground. As I got closer to the buildings, I could see a serviceman sitting outside holding a football. He wore a RAF uniform and appeared slim, even frail, as he sat there, turning the ball round in his hands. He seemed friendly enough, so I ran over to him. As I approached, he looked up at me, and a smile spread across his face. He held out the football to me and asked, "Play ball?" I nodded. He placed the ball on the ground, stood up, and kicked it over to where I was standing.

I had never kicked a football in my life. I was barefoot and had not owned a pair of shoes since I had lived with the Sisters at the orphanage, which felt like a lifetime ago. Food was my main concern—it was where I spent all my earnings—so my clothing consisted of tatters, scraps, and whatever I could manage to scrounge or steal. My small, calloused feet had carried me from city to city, running nearly the longitude of India, and now they were punting a ball back and forth with this strange yet kindly man who was the first person to take a genuine interest in me for years.

After we had played for a little while, the serviceman offered me some chocolates and sweets. I grabbed them hungrily and ate them there on the spot. I hadn't been lucky in my search for food recently, and it had been a few weeks since I'd had a decent meal. I was famished, and the sweets would tide me over until I could hopefully get something more substantial. If I played my cards right, maybe the man would give me some of his rations before I had to go find shelter for the night.

The serviceman must have enjoyed my company, for he resumed our football game and played with me until it was late in the afternoon. I remember laughing as I chased after the ball, kicking it back in his direction when he sent it flying toward the rice field where I had emerged that morning. This was the longest positive human interaction I'd had in seven years. The last people I remembered treating me this warmly were the Sisters at St. Joseph's, and certainly no adult since then had spent this many hours playing with me. Mine was a lonely, friendless existence, and I gobbled up these drops of human kindness. I was as starved for affection as I was for food.

At last, the sun started to head west. The serviceman picked up the ball and said to me, "Well, you'd better run along home now." I looked at him sadly. I understood enough English to know what he meant, and I knew I could not do as he asked. I shook my head and said, "No home. No family." He asked me where I was from, and I told him, "Jamshedpur," for that was where Mrs. Miller lived, and that was the last city name that I could remember. The rest of the cities on my wayfaring route had been a blur of bazaars, train stations, and street corners.

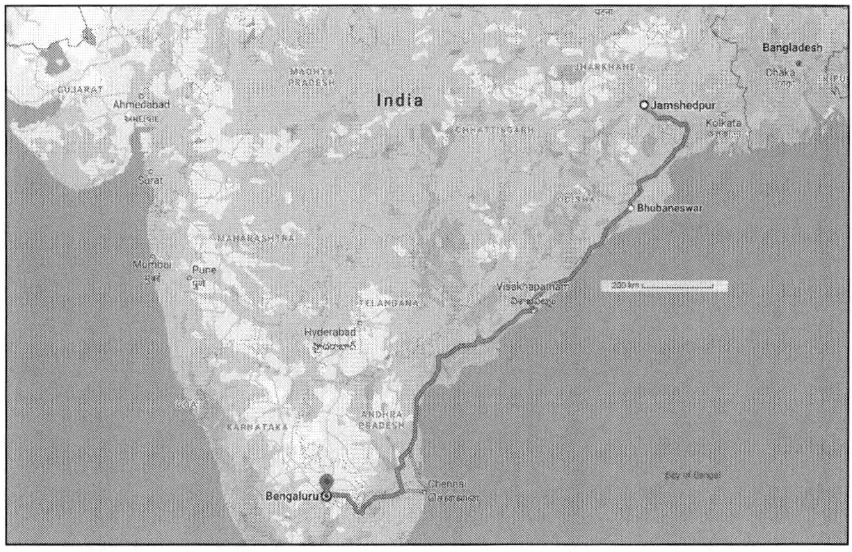

My winding five-year itinerary took me from Jamshedpur to Bangalore, following the train routes. This is the direct train route between the two cities, but my tortuous journey had far more twists and turns.

I still remember the look of shock on the man's face when I told him where I had travelled from. His eyes widened and he exclaimed, "Good Lord, that's miles and miles away!" A series of emotions played across the man's face as his surprise gave way to concern and finally determination. He said, "What is your name, lad?" I told him, "Joseph." He said, "My name is Nelson Taylor." Then he squared his jaw and said, "Right, Joseph, well you had better come with me." He reached out his hand to me. I looked at his outstretched fingers, and then I raised my eyes to his face. He didn't look angry or like he wanted to do me harm. People seldom touched me, and when they did it was rarely out of kindness, but something made me trust that this man was not going to hurt me. I tentatively reached out and placed my hand in the man's palm. He grasped my little hand in his and led me back to the Air Force barracks.

RAF barracks in India during World War II.

Nelson walked me inside one of the large buildings that I had been drawn to earlier that morning. I thought to myself, how lucky that I had chosen to run across that rice field and play ball with this man. It was looking like I would not only eat well today, but perhaps I could even get shelter for the night. It had been so long since I had been able to sleep without having to keep one eye open. I slept inside when I could, often in train stations, but I had to remain aware of my surroundings at all times. The police could arrest me for sleeping inside a public place, and other street children would steal my few paltry belongings if I weren't vigilant. What a luxury it would be if I could catch a few hours of rest inside this Air Force billet.

As we walked through the building, I saw other servicemen engaged in various activities. Some were playing cards, others were rolling dice, and some were sitting by themselves reading. Several men were gathered round a billiard table, cheering loudly as they each took shots at the pool balls. Nelson led me to the middle of the room and said, "Gentlemen, I want to introduce you to someone." Some of the men looked up, others remained engrossed with what they were doing. Nelson continued. "This lad is my ward. His name is Joseph." A few more eyes looked up in my direction. "None of you are to lay a hand on him. I will be seeing to his care." He then led me aside and said, "Stay by my side, lad. You needn't run any longer. I shall be looking after you now."

I couldn't begin to comprehend my luck. I had encountered hundreds of servicemen and British tourists along my journey, and no one else had offered to take me in or to make me their ward. It felt so arbitrary that this man should decide that my little life was worth saving. But Nelson had made the snap decision that out of all the orphans in India, I was to survive thanks to his protection. He made sure that his fellow servicemen were kind to me and didn't give me any trouble, whereas without his auspices, I might have been on the receiving end of their boot. He arranged for me to have the title of "chaiwallah," which was someone who served tea to the officers. This task gave me a purpose for residing in the billet and let me earn my keep. I did exactly as I was told. I knew that I had been given a new chance at life, and I was going to hold onto it with all the strength that my little hands could muster.

Nelson was my savior, and I followed him round the barracks like a little puppy. Wherever he went, I was right behind. I still remember the feeling of gratitude and joy when he gave me food from his rations. It was luxurious compared to the simple fare I had been used to stealing, pulling out of rubbish bins, or buying with my scant budget. I gobbled whatever he gave me and rewarded him with looks of pure adoration and loyalty. He bought me clean clothes and showed me where to shower so I could clean off the years of grime from living on the streets. At night he let me sleep in a cot next to his bed. I remember the first few nights I woke up in terror, sure I was about to be attacked, only to look over and see Nelson asleep next to me. After several days of this, I finally got my first full night's sleep in years. I felt like I had been plucked out of my precarious existence, full of danger and arbitrary abuse, and placed in the middle of a fairytale. Life was suddenly peaches and cream, and I did not want this fairytale to end.

During those first weeks at the RAF base, I didn't let Nelson out of my sight. I feared that if I strayed from him, the other servicemen might not be as tolerant of my presence. Some of the men were friendly to me and gave me sweets, but most of them would not feed me out of their own rations like Nelson did. When I was doing my duties as chaiwallah, serving the other officers their tea, I made sure to keep Nelson in the corner of my eye. I even followed him onto the airfield when he was working.

RAF airplane mechanics in India working on a De Havilland Mosquito, a lightweight twin-engine bomber aircraft, circa 1943.

Nelson was a corporal in the RAF, and his duties included being an airplane mechanic. He oversaw everything from general maintenance to repairing aircraft that had been damaged in battle. His primary job was to fix and maintain the armory sections of the RAF planes and to ensure that the bomb attachments were in working order.

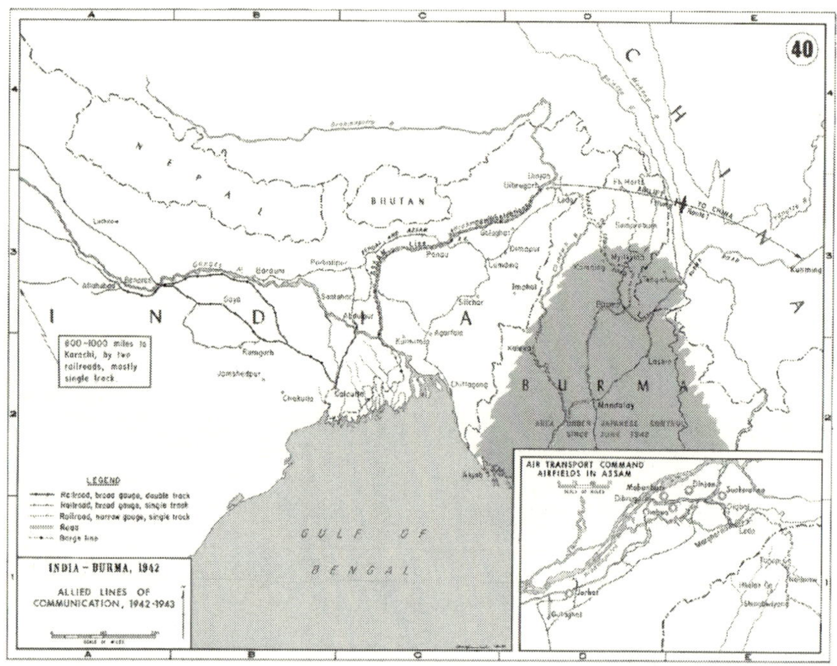

The China-Burma-India Theater of War, and the flight path over the Himalayan Mountains, aka "The Hump."

We were part of the China-Burma-India Theater of War. China was fighting on the side of the Allies against the Japanese, and in order for British and American troops in India to bring gold and supplies to the Chinese, they had to make the treacherous journey through Burma. This had made Burma a prime target for Japan, and in 1942, the Japanese army occupied the country and sent their troops to block the Burma Road, which was the main overland supply route. The Allies couldn't traverse Burma by land, but they could still cross the country by air. It fell to the RAF and the US Air Force to carry out the vital duty of flying over the eastern end of the Himalayan Mountains, which the pilots called the Hump, and carry crucial resources to China.

The RAF De Havilland Mosquito flying during World War II, circa 1944.

The RAF also sent bomber aircraft to engage the Japanese during the Burma Campaign, and I remember the wonder of seeing these airplanes flying to and from the base where Nelson was stationed. One of my clearest memories from that time is seeing a De Havilland Mosquito returning from a bombing run. The Mosquito was a light bomber aircraft made mostly of wood. It was small and only had room for a pilot and a navigator. The Mosquito I saw flying back to the base that day had been attacked by anti-aircraft guns. It had pieces of its tail shot away, and there were large holes in its fuselage, and yet it still flew, carrying its crew to safety.

I chased after Nelson as he went over to where the aircraft had landed, and I stood transfixed as he began his repairs. Watching him work on airplanes was endlessly fascinating to me. I thought perhaps one day I could be a pilot and have the freedom to fly through the sky to parts unknown. My dream of flying came sooner than I imagined it would. Nelson was called away to work at another RAF base, and he made arrangements for me to accompany him. I remember the excitement of boarding the airplane and the wonder of looking out the window as the earth dropped away. The Indian landscape shrunk below me, and I felt as though I were a giant, walking along tiny roads with miniature trees and buildings the size of matchboxes. The steady rumble of the aircraft lulled me into a light sleep, and when I opened my eyes, we had arrived at our destination. Nelson worked at this base for several days, and then we returned to Bangalore.

Most of the time, Nelson could arrange for me to come with him on these trips. However, some of his assignments were too dangerous for me to accompany him, and he saw to it that I was given lodgings and a job to do until he returned. The commanding officer for our base lived separately from the other officers in a cabin that was camouflaged amongst the trees. Nelson told me that I was to be a "babaji wallah," or a manservant. I learned how to clean the commanding officer's house, lay out his uniform for the morning, and shine his shoes. I would do this every day until Nelson returned so that I would continue to earn my keep. I was happy to do any work that Nelson told me to do. I owed him my life, and I would have gone to the moon and back if he had asked me.

Unbeknownst to me, the rhythms of my happy life with Nelson were about to change. It was the spring of 1945, and the Burma Campaign was drawing its last ugly breaths. Throughout the billets, the RAF officers were talking eagerly about the increasing likelihood of demobilization. I could feel the tense excitement in the air as the officers realized they would soon be able to return home to their families. I didn't know what this would mean for me, I just knew that I wanted to follow Nelson wherever he might go. One day he came to me and said, "Joseph, how would you like to go with me to England?" At the time, I didn't know the difference between England and Timbuktu. I told him, "Yes, I like to go with you," even though I had no idea what England was. Nelson smiled and said, "Splendid, you shall come to England with me, and you shall be my son." Little did I know the lengths to which Nelson would have to go in order to make that promise a reality.

CHAPTER 4

Nelson soon realized that he had his work cut out for him. It wouldn't be so easy to adopt this little orphaned Indian boy. Shortly after I had met him outside the RAF barracks on that fateful January day, I confessed to him, "A woman named Mrs. Miller adopted me, but I ran away. I don't want to go back there." He asked me why, and I told him, "She hit me every day. She tried to kill me, so I ran." Nelson seemed deeply troubled by this. He was a kind and profoundly empathetic man, and he felt other people's pain as if it were his own. A lesser man might have washed his hands of me once he learned that I was already adopted and sent me back to that life of captivity. Nelson understood that if I had chosen life on the streets over life with Mrs. Miller, she must be a monster indeed.

Unbeknownst to me, Nelson had set his mind on adopting me and bringing me with him to England as soon as he had chosen to take me on as his ward. However, now that he knew that I belonged to Mrs.

Miller, this task would be more difficult. He would need to track her down and ask her to relinquish her claim on me. I was able to give him the clues he needed to find her. I described Mrs. Miller's estate in Jamshedpur and the squalid horrors I had been forced to endure there. When he asked me about my life before Mrs. Miller, I told him of the Sisters at St. Joseph's orphanage and the loving kindness they had shown me. Armed with the knowledge that I had been adopted from a Catholic orphanage, Nelson reached out to the RAF chaplain who served his jurisdiction, Reverend B. T. Buckley. He described the situation to Reverend Buckley. He explained that he wished to adopt me but did not know if he was within his legal rights to do so. Reverend Buckley contacted St. Mary's Church in Jamshedpur on Nelson's behalf to enquire if any of the priests there could contact Mrs. Miller. Lo and behold, he received the following reply, written on 21st January 1945 from the Jesuit priest, Father J. Comerford. (Original letter on pages 170-171.)

> Dear Fr. Buckley,
>
> I am glad to get news of that boy Joseph Miller. His history is the following: He was adopted by a certain Mr. and Mrs. Miller (Catholics) of Golmuri, Jamshedpur and up to about a year or two ago proved incorrigible. Mrs. Miller shed tears in my presence at what she called this boy's ingratitude. He couldn't be corrected for he would abscond for a day or more. If sent on a message to buy household needs he would spend a much longer time than needed with the Indian bazaar brats and then had a habit of nipping a few coins from the sum he

received for the purchases. (I think she also referred to a gambling propensity). At any rate he was punished, absconded and she let him stay away. I made enquiries and found no trace. I thought that he was still somewhere in my neighborhood.

This boy Joseph is an adopted son of Mrs. Miller given to her by the Chandernagore Convent when a baby. Mrs. Miller will be pleased to hear that he is being cared for and follows the Catholic faith. She will make no claim on him. Accordingly whoever has won the youngster's good will and is prepared to train him and to educate him as a Catholic may assume the full title of guardian. Besides if my register records him which I doubt, there is a Joseph Miller born 4th May 1926 but no reference to adoption. This date makes him far too old. His baptismal record is probably to be found in St. Joseph's Convent Chandernagore as the nuns have a crèche for little orphan children and doubtless baptize them as soon as they receive their tiny charges.

If then the RAF man has taken to him and the boy responds, you will probably agree with me to let this youngster continue in his charge is a splendid solution. If you be good enough to let me know something of the youngster even in his future career I shall be very pleased. Mrs. Miller too will be quite delighted to know that what she found impossible someone else has succeeded in. She was fond of this boy but had to relinquish all claim to him when he proved so insubordinate in her care.

Are you this same Fr. Buckley who was attached to this Catholic parish or are you straight from Europe?

With all good wishes fully reciprocated and I shall not forget to offer for you a prayer or memento at holy mass for success in your difficult work.

Yours sincerely in Our Lord

J. Comerford, S.J.

I had been right to fear Mrs. Miller's pursuit after I had run away. She clearly had not stopped wishing she could get her hands on me. She had instructed this priest, Father Comerford, to make enquiries about my whereabouts after I had fled. Luckily, it appeared that she had waited to tell him of my disappearance, which gave me a head start in my escape, since he seemed to believe that I had run away only a year or two before.

She had spun other lies about me too, telling Father Comerford that I had been incorrigible and insubordinate. It was true that I had occasionally taken a few coins from the change I received at the bazaar, but it was only to buy food to keep from starving on the days that she decided not to feed me.

Reverend Buckley must have relayed this letter to Nelson, informing him that Mrs. Miller had abandoned her claim on me. In reading this letter now, I feel immensely grateful and fortunate that Nelson was the kind of man who could see through her description of me. She couldn't possess me any longer, but she couldn't help trying to defame my character before she let me go.

Now that I was in the clear to be adopted, Father Buckley and Nelson wrote to St. Joseph's Convent in Chandannagar to track down the records of my baptism. Mother Superior Marie Agnes still remembered me and replied with the following pair of letters, written in the beginning of April 1945. (Original letters on page 172.)

Dear Reverend Father,

In answer to your letter I shall try and tell you as much as I can gather from our Register about the Boy in question.

His Mother was a Bengalee and his Father is said to be a pure European. The Mother died and left her son to a Bengalee friend who brought him to our Orphanage when he was 3 years old. He was taken over on the 15th August 1935 and was baptised "Joseph" on the 20th August '35. Mrs. Miller, an Anglo-Indian lady from Tatanagar called at our Indian Orphanage in view of adopting a child and took a great fancy to Joe. He left with her on the 12th June 1938 and we heard nothing more about him.

Joseph seemed quite out of place with the other little Indian children in our Orphanage and we were so pleased when Mrs. Miller gave him a Home.

I am very pleased to know that Joseph is now in a good College and hope and pray he will give every satisfaction.

May I recommend our Community and Boarding School to your good prayers.

Yours respectfully in J.C.

Mother Marie Agnes, Superior

Dear Corporal Taylor,

I am pleased to do my best to tell you all I know of the little boy in question. He came to us on the 15th August 1935, and seemed to be at least 3 years of age, he was able to run about everywhere and had to be watched continually. He may of course have been only two years old. He was baptised on the 20th August and was called Joseph. He remained with us for about a year and then Mrs. Miller took a great fancy to him and asked to adopt him.

Joseph's Mother was a pure Indian and the Father a European, either English or Scotch. When we take over a child into our Orphanage he cannot be reclaimed and therefore we make very few inquiries about the parentage.

I thank you for your very nice letter and I hope Joseph will always be grateful and repay you for all your kindness.

Yours sincerely

Mother Marie Agnes, Superior

Dear Mother Marie Agnes, how she and the other Sisters had loved and cared for me, only to be tricked into giving me away. Reading this letter now, I genuinely believe that they did not know that Mrs. Miller's intentions were to make me her servant. They likely thought her interest in me was that of a mother wishing to give a good home to one of India's multitudes of orphans. Five of my formative childhood years had been spent on the run from that woman, travelling restlessly from city to city, in constant danger and terrified of capture. While fate had ultimately delivered me into the hands of Nelson, what a harrowing journey it had been to get there.

Nelson himself wrote to Father Comerford, explaining his intention to adopt me and assuring the priest that he would continue to raise me in the Catholic faith. Nelson had been christened in the Church of England; however, he respected my Catholic baptism and was committed to providing me with religious continuity. Nelson was a remarkable man and had an intrinsic respect for the autonomy of all human beings. He was not in the business of forcing his beliefs on anyone and would no more try to convert a little Indian orphan than he would any of his countrymen. On 6th April, Father Comerford penned a reply. (Original letter on page 173.)

> Dear Corporal Taylor
>
> I am more than gratified at hearing your account and your intentions regarding Joe Miller. I am convinced that he will prove grateful to you for all you are doing for him. You ought to remind him not to let die a spark of gratitude for his first adopting parents—Mr. and Mrs. Miller. They brought him up from babyhood and treated him as their own child. They supplied all his needs and such personal efforts should not be without a response in this recipient. Mrs. Miller shed tears in my presence when she had to relinquish all hope of controlling the boy. She will be very pleased to hear that he is safe.
>
> I made enquiries about him around here and I was about to examine a locality where he was last seen when this letter reached me that he had been taken on by you. Now I shall

convey your message to Mr. and Mrs. Miller who will be indeed pleased to know that Joe will be educated and brought up in his Catholic faith.

With all good wishes.

Yours sincerely,

J. Comerford, SJ

It was a miracle that Mrs. Miller had relinquished her claim on me. She would send no more men in search of my whereabouts. Father Comerford's language was oddly revealing. Mrs. Miller had shed tears not because she missed me as an adoptive mother should, but rather because she would no longer be able to control me as her property. I was free. I would never again have to run from place to place to avoid capture. I would not have to sleep on the street, or steal to survive, or be friendless and alone.

Nelson was now at liberty to begin the adoption process, and on 26th April, he wrote to the Society for the Protection of Children in Calcutta to make a formal request. At the time, India was a British colony, and it adhered to British law on such matters as adoptions. Nelson did not want to jeopardize my chances, so he followed the legal procedure to the letter. On 7th May, he received the following reply. (Original letter on page 174.)

Dear Mr. Taylor,

Thank you for your letter of the 26th ultimo regarding the above-named boy. We have placed on record the particulars supplied by you which are much the same as obtained by us from the Convent direct.

We have been assured by the Convent that there is no claimant for the boy, and we therefore see no objection to your adopting him and arranging for his welfare as outlined in your original letter to us.

We shall nevertheless welcome periodical reports regarding the boy's progress and welfare if you can possibly arrange this.

With all good wishes,

Yours sincerely,

General Secretary

Looking back at the amount of work that Nelson put into securing my adoption, it was clear that he couldn't bear the thought of leaving me behind. I didn't know it at the time, but before we met, Nelson had been captured by the Japanese as a prisoner of war. After the Japanese occupied Burma in 1942, Allied troops tried to retake the country to maintain overland trade with allied China. Many of our soldiers were captured by the Japanese and forced to work in slave labour camps, and Nelson was among them. I do not know the horrors that he must have endured, for he never spoke to me about that period of his life, but I can imagine that his experience as a POW may have been similar to the fictionalized barbarism depicted in *The Bridge on the River Kwai.*

The Japanese officers who ran the POW camps in Burma were nearly as savage as the Nazis who orchestrated the better-known atrocities of the Holocaust. British, Dutch, Australian, and American prisoners were forced at gunpoint to build the Burma-Siam railway in order to make Burma easier for the Japanese military to traverse. During construction, nearly 13,000 POWs died and were buried in shallow graves along the railway's path. Many succumbed to starvation or disease, and hundreds more were beaten to death or shot by prison guards.

Prisoners of war building the Burma-Siam "Death Railway." Nelson was a POW like these men, forced at gunpoint to labour until he was nearly dead.

I do not know how Nelson escaped the horrific fate that befell many of his captured countrymen. There were some prison camps in Burma that were liberated by the Allies during the War, and Nelson may have been in one of these. Or perhaps he was one of the lucky few who were able to sneak through barbed wire in the cover of night and trek hundreds of miles through the jungle to the relative safety of China. Whatever his path to freedom, Nelson had escaped a fate worse than death. He made it back to India, a gaunt shadow of the man who had enlisted in the RAF at the start of the War.

His experiences as a POW must have helped him empathize with the life I had led on the streets, running from the horrors of captivity and servitude. As soon as he received word that I was legally able to be adopted, Nelson wrote to his parents, Albert and Nora, and introduced the idea of bringing me with him to England. He told them my story and impressed upon them the precariousness of my little life. He had become my sole protector and my lifeline. Nelson uniquely understood how dire my situation had been before we found each other, and he knew that if he left me behind in India, I would have little choice but to return to a life of grinding poverty and danger lurking round every corner.

Albert and Nora were quick to give Nelson their full support in his efforts to adopt me. They would help in any way they could to bring me home. Albert made a phone call to the Air Ministry to learn what might need to be done on his part to ensure that I would be able to return to England with Nelson. On 20th May, Albert typed a letter to Nelson, reassuring him that he was making every effort to facilitate the adoption process. (Original letter on pages 175.)

> My Dear Son,
>
> I wrote to you on Tuesday last but we had another letter from you yesterday, it was here when I arrived home from work, dated 9th May, with the two snaps enclosed. Old Lad you look tired & sad and it is not very cheering to see you looking

like that. I should think that it is nearly time that you were hearing about coming home yourself, just how do you stand on the list now Son? Have you any idea?

I have had no news yet from Welfare but have every hopes. Do your best to let me have that information about you & Joey as soon please Son and then I shall be able to 'gatecrash' into their hives again without waiting for them to send for me.

I guess that you feel a bit 'fed' now that the news from here of war is finished but I do not think that your area will supply war news for a lot longer. Never fear Old Son we keep our mind very much on your Area News, it is true that we do not get so much of it splashed across the paper headlines but there are some thousands of people at home with relatives out your way who are eager for what little is doled out for us to read.

Mum was looking down at her strawberries just before lunch and is already talking about how much jam she will be able to make against you two coming home, Lord Woolton approving. I say that because there is a lot of talk of a cut in the sugar ration, heaven knows that we do not get overburdened with sweetstuffs as it is but I suppose that we must think of the poor Germans who will have to go without if we do not accept a cut. That, perhaps, is an unfair thing to say but it seems odd to me that we have managed pretty well so far but as soon as the war in Europe is finished so a shortage occurs in many of the essentials. Roll on that Election perhaps then we shall be able to put things right but I've almost given up hope for this country, cant and vested interest appear to be pretty rife. I can only hope that you Lads will be strong enough to make yourselves heard when you return.

The next day, Albert received the following letter, written on 18th May, from the Air Ministry regarding my adoption. When he read this letter, Albert realized that adopting me would be more challenging than he and Nelson had originally believed. According to British law, an adoptive parent had to be at least twenty-one years older than their ward. Based on the year of my baptism, my age was determined to be ten at the time, although I was likely closer to thirteen. Nelson, however, was at most only twelve years my senior. Therefore, he would not be eligible to adopt me. It would have to be Albert and Nora, a world away in England, who were listed as my adoptive parents, which would significantly complicate matters. (Original letter on page 176.)

Dear Sir,

With reference to your call on the 12th instant and our conversation regarding the adopted boy of your son, I think we should advise you that, as I understand the English law, legal adoption cannot be effected unless there is a difference of not less than 21 years between the ages of your son and the boy. I believe that English law applies to India but it would be as well for your son to look into this aspect of his problem, as, if legal adoption cannot be arranged it may alter the whole situation.

When your son returns to the U.K. I do not think there will be any difficulty about bringing the boy with him and if he applies to the Command through his Commanding Officer they would probably embark the boy on the same vessel.

The boy would require documents in order to enter the U.K. and your Son should get in touch with the Home Department of the Provincial Government in which he is stationed who would issue the necessary passport or identity documents etc. Although the boy is a British subject he must be in possession of these papers before embarking so they must be obtained in India.

As regards the fare, if the boy is permitted to travel home in the same troopship as your son and is provided with third class accommodation the cost of the passage at half rate would be £17.10.

Civilians, however, are not normally permitted to travel third class on troopships and if the boy returns unaccompanied the cost of his fare at 2nd class rates would be £23.10.

As the airman is unmarried he is precluded from the grant of a passage at public expense.

Perhaps I should point out again that the important problem at the moment is the legal [age] of the boy, as the above remarks would not apply if the courts refuse the application, in which case I do not think there would be any prospect of bringing the boy to England. If I can be of any further assistance, please do not hesitate to get in touch with me.

Yours faithfully,

D. V. Tandy

Albert hastily added to his letter from the previous day, informing Nelson of the potentially bad news. (Original letter on page 177.)

> Monday, 21st May, '45.
>
> As you can see, I did not finish this yesterday so here I am again. I did not expect that there would be a Post delivery this morning but there was one and I had a letter from welfare and I'll make a copy and enclose it with this. One piece of the info is a little disturbing, but you must take up enquiries right away and let me know the result. The point in question is the difference in age and if that is a difficulty I think that you had better name us as the person [who will adopt Joe] and I'll give you full power to act for me but be careful as the snag about getting him to this country may present more difficulties. Anyhow I'll leave it to you to act as you think best but you have my permission to use my name as far as you think fit in order to get this laddie settled with a view to him coming to this country.
>
> I think that this is about all for this week Son, so I will close down for now. Let me have some info as soon as you possibly can. Cheerio Old Son, God Bless You and take care of you. All at Home send Love and best wishes. Cheerio! Happy Landings! Dad

Nelson and Albert were beginning to realize that adopting me was going to be all hands on deck. This would be an international rescue mission that would require the coordinated efforts of Nelson, Albert, and anyone with governmental connections that Albert could enlist.

The Taylors would need all the help they could get to cut through the ever-multiplying layers of bureaucratic red tape. Despite the increasing challenges, Nelson was steadfast in his promise to me. He was not going to leave me behind. Even if he had to row me in a boat himself, he was going to do whatever it took to bring me home to the new life that awaited me in England.

CHAPTER 5

The window of opportunity for bringing me to England was closing more rapidly by the day. Nelson would soon be demobilized, and since he could not adopt me and bring me to England himself, he and Albert would have to coordinate a rescue mission that could take place in Nelson's absence. There were many pieces to organize in this game of chess that reached halfway round the globe. By now it was May 1945, and it was becoming increasingly clear that an Allied victory against the Axis powers in Europe was at hand. Hitler had ended his life as April drew to a close, effectively cutting off the head of the Axis war machine. In the days that followed, German forces across Europe surrendered, and the Allied world erupted in celebration. Now it was only a matter of time before the surviving troops would return home and try to reassemble the lives that had been fractured by war.

Nelson knew that it was no longer feasible to keep me with him at the RAF base in Bangalore. Reverend Buckley arranged for me to be housed off-site in a nearby orphanage so that Nelson could continue to check up on me. I was deeply attached to this man who was the first person to care for me as his own child, and when I was placed in the orphanage, I descended into a deep despair. I had been given a taste of loving kindness, and then suddenly it was ripped away. Life once again felt unstable and filled with arbitrary cruelty. When Nelson visited me in the orphanage, he could read my misery loud and clear. This institution was no place for his child. I needed the security of a family. While he couldn't house me himself, he could still find me a home.

During his years of service, Nelson had befriended British colonial families living in India, and he turned to them now and entreated their aid. He knew that he needed to find someone who would be responsible for providing me with shelter and care. He would see to it that they were well compensated for taking me in, of course, and he would ensure that my expenses were paid for while I was in their custody. He wanted to be certain that this surrogate family would foster me as their own little boy while I lived with them. He had a legitimate concern that if the family treated me like a servant, I would become despondent again and feel that my only recourse was to run away. In order for this rescue operation to work, Nelson needed to be confident in my whereabouts at all times.

Friends in Shillong in the northeast of India answered Nelson's plea and offered to take me in. These were good friends, and Nelson trusted them, but what a journey that would be! Shillong was a week's trip from Bangalore, over 3,000 kilometres. Looking at the route on a map, the irony is not lost on me that in travelling to Shillong, I would be retracing much of the path that I forged in my flight from Mrs. Miller. This time, however, I would be riding on the inside of the train with a proper ticket in hand.

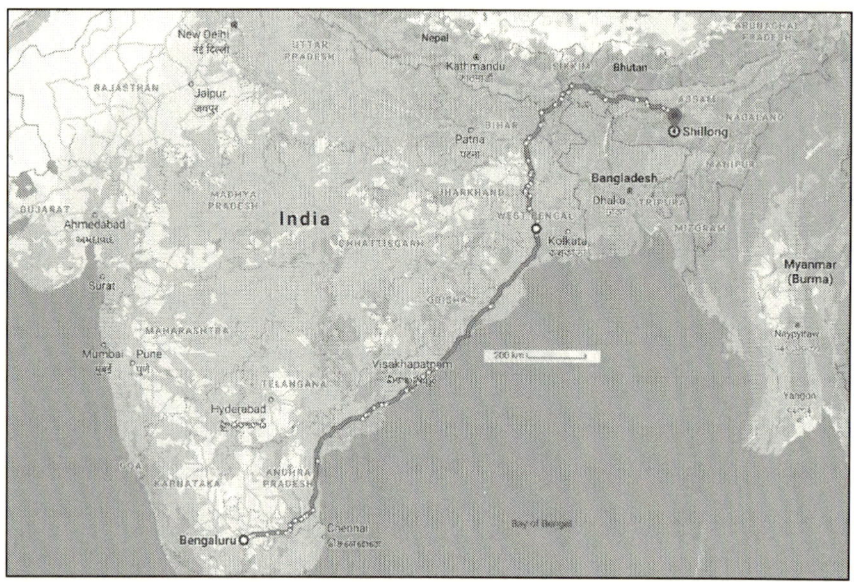

My 3,000 kilometre journey from Bangalore to Shillong was my first time traveling on the inside of a train.

When I arrived in Shillong, my foster family welcomed me and made me feel at home. They were an English couple with a daughter named Jane. I don't remember much about the time I spent with them, but according to letters that Nelson sent to Albert, Jane and I became fast friends. During the time I spent with the family, Nelson explained that I was to work diligently to improve my English. At the time, I spoke only rudimentary English. I picked up most of what I knew from interacting with Nelson and his fellow British servicemen. Mind you, I also spoke seven distinct Indian dialects, which I had learned as I trekked my way southward through different geographical and linguistic regions. Now English would become my mother tongue, and I would need all the practice I could get in order to communicate with my new family in London.

Albert was also making arrangements for me to attend primary school when I arrived in England. He and Nelson were determined that I should receive a proper education, so I would need to start learning my subjects as soon as possible. I'd had little to no formal schooling up to this point. It is possible that the Sisters at St. Joseph's had introduced me to reading and writing while I was in their care. The convent was also a school, and the nuns had a duty to teach their young charges. However, during my years on the run, I had lost any education that they might have bestowed on me. To prepare me for the life that lay ahead of me as a British citizen, Reverend Buckley came to the rescue and helped Nelson enroll me in St. Edmund's College in Shillong. He ensured that I would receive a complementary education so that Nelson could afford to send me. On 14th June, Father J. I. O'Leary, the Principal of St. Edmund's College, penned the following letter to Nelson. (Original letter on page 178.)

> Dear sir,
>
> Your letter dated the 5th instant received.

We agreed with the Rev. Father (Captain) Buckley to give Joe Miller a free place in this school. We shall not therefore charge him any fees.

Other expenses such as books, stationary, you may kindly pay. A bill will be sent you, for any such charge.

Yours sincerely,

J. I. O'Leary

P.S. He is an intelligent boy and is making good progress.

Reverend Buckley had taken it upon himself to become my champion. He saw to it that there was money for my room and board and my personal effects. Nelson was living on a military salary, and servicemen of his rank earned only a few pounds per month. All these expenses added up, and without Reverend Buckley's help, Nelson would not have been able to afford to provide for me while I was in Shillong. This plan did not go off without a hitch, however, much to Reverend Buckley's dismay. Nelson informed the Reverend that a local priest, Father Ricaldone, had refused to coordinate the disbursal of the money that had been allocated to me. With much exasperation, Reverend Buckley wrote to Nelson on 15th June, and promised to intercede on my behalf. (Original letter on pages 179-180.)

Dear Cpl. Taylor,

Your letter has just arrived, it has taken ten days: nearly twice as long as a letter from Blighty. From the above, you see I have been posted. I was on my way to the old Wing when, in passing through Calcutta, I heard of my posting here.

I am very upset by your letter, by the refusal of Fr. Ricaldone to hand over the money and half of the kit with Joe. I am just waiting to hear whether another Catholic RAF chaplain has been sent to Shillong, as was expected of Fr. White whose health is poor; but if he has not gone there, I shall consider Shillong still within the bounds of my jurisdiction; and therefore I shall visit the place as soon as possible. While up there I shall thrash out matters in no vague terms with both the Bishop and Fr. Ricaldone and see that Joe gets satisfaction. Should Fr. White be posted there, I shall send a letter to the Bishop with a copy to Fr. Ricaldone and ask for immediate action; failing which, I shall write to the Superior Provincial of the Salesians—a friend of mine—and get him to step in. He must have understood the initial amount to be a voluntary donation, that is feasible, but that the boy's kit should be considered common property is just a little far-fetched. However, I shall demand 150 rupees plus the complete outfit. It is surprising that Fr. Ricaldone has not written to me.

Hoping matters will straighten out concerning Joe and that you will have the pleasure of taking him home with you soon.

I remain,

Yours sincerely in Our Lord

B. T. Buckley

Nelson meanwhile wrote several more letters to Albert, keeping him apprised of my situation. The rescue operation was going forward as planned, and if all the pieces lined up just right, I would be coming home within a matter of months. There were still many pieces left to maneuver into place before this international game of chess could be won. The anxiety that Albert clearly perceived in Nelson's letters was due in no small part to the difficulties that Nelson was having with securing money for my living expenses. His plan hinged on his ability to pay for my keep until he could arrange for my passage to England. On 25th June, Albert replied and reassured Nelson that he and I would have the support we needed. The whole family was prepared to help in any way they could. (Original letter on pages 181-183.)

My Dear Son,

We have had two letters from you this week and the packet containing Joey's letters. The letters were dated 15th June and 18th June respectively. Someone is obviously pulling a finger out in the matter of mail coming in this direction, I wish that the same could be said about mail coming out to you. However I suppose that it will all right itself one day but roll on that day when we shall not have to write you.

You gave me quite a shock in the first of these letters, with the postscript from Jane. I began to think that you had started a nursery or some such but the second letter cleared the air a little and I assume that Jane is a friend of Joey's.

Well Old Lad we were pleased to hear that the parcel had arrived safely, I was a little worried about it as we read so much of packets for the Far East 'going astray' and not arriving at their destination. So you are pleased with the parcel. I'm glad that it has pleased you. I'll get all that I can for you but unless you ask I shall not dispatch any more for a while. We have a lovely little Flannel Suit here for him. I think that I mentioned this in a previous letter, and Mum is well away with the pullover but if you want it sent you must say. You see Son, in spite of you volunteering for that extra year, we both think that you will be home before that time and we do not want to send parcels out with you on the way home. Understand?

Now Old Lad about this money question. I want to try to explain my outlook and maybe it will be a little difficult to put into this letter but I want you to understand that at all times, as far as I am concerned your happiness and peace of mind are my first consideration, that is as far as you are concerned. This money must not be allowed to worry you at all and it is there for you to use as YOU think fit. Joan is away for this weekend but as soon as she can manage, I'll get her to put a further £10 to the credit of Mr. Mellish but I have a further suggestion to make to you and I'd like an answer as soon as you can let me have it. Would you like me to put a larger sum, say £50 to your credit out at one of the banks in India. It is only a suggestion and to my mind it would appear to have several advantages. By this means you would always have a sense of security where cash is concerned and a means of not worrying yourself about getting from home. After all Son, you are free, white & 21 and therefore quite capable of thinking for yourself and it is YOUR MONEY that you are dealing with. I don't want you to think that I do not want the trouble of dealing with these affairs for you but Old Lad as far as possible I want to stop you worrying. Your last letter is very much like a youngster asking for a penny to spend and I want you to get above that. I'm not condemning you for that so please don't let that enter your mind. Money is only useful for the happiness it will bring, think that out sometime, that is my outlook on money and if it will serve that purpose then use it and don't worry. I hope that I have made that clear without giving you cause to grieve but if you do feel a little annoyed, well Lad go back to the beginning of this paragraph and read that again. O.K?

I expect that you will wonder how your sister Joan enters into the question of remitting money out to you. Well she has a banking account with the National & Provincial at Tooting Broadway and that is the easiest way of dealing with this problem. I get Mum to draw out from the P.O. account and pay Joan back that way. I am friendly with the Manager of this branch, he is Treasurer to the Unit Committee and is always ready to help all he can in these matters. The first remittances I sent were sent during the time I had the Unit's account under my signature but that is no longer the case and I'm very glad about it as I'll explain to you when I see you and when we get a chance for a 'gabfest'.

We have had some lovely weather during the last week, almost like Summer. I don't know how long it will last but we are trying to make the most of it whilst we can. We had tea outside this evening and I generally manage to have my final snack out there before going to bed.

Mum has been very busy of late bottling fruit and making jam. I think that I mentioned that once before in a letter to you. She has quite a store of these now but the trouble about them is that she counts them each day so there is no chance of getting away anything. They are all stored for 'Sonny & Joey' which, as you must agree, is very poor consolation to a starving man. Well when you get back, I'll help you out for I feel sure that you will only make yourselves ill trying to eat it all or will you? I see that there is another 3lb of Loganberry Jam ready for the 'Old Oak Chest' to-morrow morning.

I am improving with my typing, I can use two fingers now but I have to be careful which two. Somebody at times gets busy mixing the letters on the keyboard with the result that the letters come out wrong as no doubt you've noticed but I get over it. (That's my excuse and I'm stcking to it) You see what I mean, someone has pinched the 'I' just when I wanted it.

Well Old Lad, I'm afraid that this is all for the week, I see that there is not a lot of paper left. When you write to Joey give him our Love and tell him I'll try to find time to write to him personally but that we are both looking forward to having him here with us and that he cannot get here too soon to suit me. Incidentally I take it that you would wish me to keep these letters of his for you so I'll put them away safe in one of the draws of my desk.

Good Night Old Son, God Bless You and take care of you. We all send Love and Best Wishes including some that you do not know or rather you have not met but who are looking forward to meeting you.

Cheerio Son! Happy Landings!

Dad

CHAPTER 6

Beneath his reassuring demeanor, Albert knew that the family would need outside help in order to secure my passage to England. There was simply too much bureaucracy standing in between me and my new life with the Taylors. The only way to cut through that much governmental red tape was to entreat the aid of someone with deep connections in the government, and Albert knew just the man. He reached out to his friend and colleague, Mr. Leslie Brooks, a kind-hearted gentleman who I would come to know as Uncle Leslie.

Leslie Brooks had friends in all the right places, and he called on this network now, for time was of the essence. Albert needed to speed the adoption process that would make himself and Nora my legal guardians. He had to ensure that I would have my passport and travel documents in order before the autumn, when I would likely set sail. I think Uncle Leslie would have adopted me himself if it had come to that. It was extraordinary that I had such allies on my side, fighting for my survival. After all of the death and loss that they had experienced during the War, perhaps saving a life was a way for them to find meaning and hope in a world turned upside down.

Meanwhile in India, the legal wheels were turning slowly. On 6 July, The Society for the Protection of Children wrote to Nelson to reassure him that the adoption process was moving forward. (Original letter on page 184.)

> Dear Mr. Taylor,
>
> I am sorry for the delay in replying to your letter in the matter of the above-named boy earlier. The letter was unfortunately mislaid by the office, and hence this delay. I was interested to hear of the developments in the case.
>
> Having regard to the circumstances you have alluded to we sincerely trust that your endeavours to take the boy with you to England will be successful. Should, however, the case be otherwise, we shall certainly do all we can to accede to your request. We, nevertheless, feel that the Society's intervention will not be called for and that you will be able to overcome the difficulties you are at the moment confronted with.
>
> We are glad to know that Joe is progressing favourably and shall welcome further reports from you in that regard from time to time.
>
> With every good wish,
>
> Yours sincerely,
>
> General Secretary

Thanks to the diligent work of Albert, Nelson, and Uncle Leslie, my passport application had been received and was being processed. On 16th July, A. I. Bowman, the Deputy Commissioner in Shillong, wrote to Wing Commander Snell, who was Nelson's Wing Commander in Bangalore, to explain the final steps that had to be completed for me to receive my passport. (Original letter on page 185.)

To The Wing Commander Snell

7082 Servicing Echelon

C/O R.A.F. Post, Bangalore

Subject: Cpl. Taylor

Sir,

I have been approached by Corporal Taylor with an application for a passport for Joseph Miller, a boy who is in Corporal Taylor's care. I understand that the boy was living with Corporal Taylor unit, as a 'chawalla', and was later put in an orphanage, on the instigation of the Unit Padre. As the boy was not happy there, Corporal Taylor took him out, and arranged for him to live with people in Shillong. I should be grateful if you would confirm this.

Corporal Taylor now wishes to take the boy to live with his parents in the United Kingdom. As there are no papers to show that the boy has been legally adopted, the passport cannot be issued in the normal way. The boy is a British Indian subject, and in order to issue a passport, we must be satisfied that Corporal Taylor has sufficient means to maintain him, and to repatriate him, if this should be necessary. I must therefore ask for guarantees on these two heads from Corporal Taylor, and these must be approved by his commanding officer. I should be grateful if you would ask Corporal Taylor to furnish such guarantees on affidavit, and would send them to me with your approval.

Your obedient servant,

A. I. Bowman, Esqr., I.C.S.

Deputy Commissioner, K & J Hills, Shillong

A handwritten note accompanied this letter. (Original letter on page 186.)

The above named airman has been responsible for the maintenance and provision of education for a young Anglo-Indian boy for some time, which has been done at the request of the airman's parents who wish to adopt the child. As his tour is nearly complete the airman wishes to make arrangements for the child to accompany him to the U.K.

His father, Mr. A. H. Taylor, contacted R.A.F. Welfare in London and the attached letter is a copy of that received by him. From this it can be seen that the question is a legal one. The airman was given to understand by the Legal Adviser in Calcutta that no adoption paper as under English Law could be effected in India, but that a form of adoption could be made, making the airman the child's guardian. This the airman has effected.

The question now arises as to whether this state of guardianship is sufficient under Indian Law to allow the child to accompany the airman, as the child is also too young to travel alone, being only nine years of age.

In such circumstances information is needed to ascertain to whom the passage money should be paid.

As summer waned, Nelson wrote one last letter to Father J. Comerford, informing the priest of my progress, and letting him know that if all went according to plan, I would soon be leaving for England. In his reply, which he penned on 17th August, Father Comerford couldn't resist getting in a jab or two at my expense. Though perhaps he was beginning to question the narrative that Mrs. Miller had concocted. His letter, which he wrote just half a month before the end of World War II, is also an interesting snapshot of a turning point in world history, as Nazism crumbled, and the new threat of Communism loomed on the horizon. The Independence Movement in India was on the cusp of winning its 90-year battle against the British Raj. Only two years later, India would declare its independence thanks to the leadership of Mahatma Gandhi, ending nearly 200 years of British rule. In the process, India would be cleaved in two in a bloody division, splintering into the rival countries of India and Pakistan. To someone like Father Comerford, it must indeed have seemed like the world was turning upside down. (Original letter on pages 187-188.)

Dear Mr. Taylor,

I am pleased to receive so excellent an account of Joe. He appears to be quite another boy from this rascal familiar to me through Mrs. Miller. Things have speeded up since you wrote and now you are beginning to get ready to move westwards. I don't believe that there will be delay in the occupation of the remaining territories.

I got a notice from the Censor department that a snapshot you mentioned in your letter was not enclosed. Perhaps you forgot it. I did receive a photo of Joey and it lies just by my ink pot. He looks quite a good little fellow, and convey to him my congratulations at his success and my hope that he will ever prove grateful to you for what you have done.

Probably Joey will never want to see India again. And I should approve. This is a country where ministers of the Gospel are needed but it's not a country where Europeans should seek careers. Australia and New Zealand are under populated and these places have a European population and can support many more.

I am greatly afraid that Communism is going to spread in the world and its class hatred and its godlessness are not going to heal the wounds of society. Its leaning over towards a better condition for the workman is agreed to by all good men. Unemployment is a stain upon a nation. Every man has a right to live, to lead a life in accord with his nature, to rear a family and to have the means of support sure. Industries unfortunately don't give this security and I fear are not going to disburse in the future years. The normal life for a man is to possess land and to be able to produce and to sell his surplus. The world is topsy turvy.

Yours sincerely,

J. Comerford, S.J.

On 2nd September 1945, representatives of the Empire of Japan signed an agreement of surrender aboard the *USS Missouri*, officially putting an end to World War II. The War had raged for six years and consumed more than 70 million lives. In the United Kingdom, nearly half a million soldiers and civilians had perished, and those who survived returned to a jagged, unfamiliar landscape of bombed out buildings and tightly controlled ration books.

Nelson would be demobilized any day now, and since he legally could not bring me with him aboard his ship, it became his top priority to find a guardian who could accompany me on my sea voyage to England. He put an advertisement in the Calcutta Statesman on 28th September, and shortly thereafter, he received the following reply from Miss Kathleen Mabert, a missionary from Scotland who had performed her religious duties in China and was now residing in the Y.W.C.A. in Calcutta. (Original letter on page 189.)

> In reference to your advertisement in the Statesman dated September 28th I shall be glad to offer my services in taking charge of the little boy travelling to the U.K. in return for help with passage. I have already been in touch with the shipping people and I am still waiting to obtain a passage.
>
> I shall be glad to give you all other particulars should you approve of my application.
>
> Yours faithfully,
>
> (Miss) K. Mabert

Nelson replied to Miss Mabert several weeks later on 11th October. He gave her a detailed job description to ensure that she was fit to oversee my care throughout the journey. He would be demobilized any day now, so if Miss Mabert were not up to the task, he wanted to have enough time to seek out another guardian. In reading his letter, I am struck by the way that he described my Indian heritage. This attitude was normal at the time, of course, and he meant nothing by it. Statements that we would now consider racist would not have raised an eyebrow in 1945. (Original letter on pages 190-193.)

> Dear Madam,
>
> I have received your reply to my advertisement in the Personal Column of the Calcutta "Statesman". I shall be glad to let you know the further particulars you require.
>
> I am a conscripted airman serving a tour of duty in this country which tour is now all but completed. During my travels I adopted as my ward a little orphan child to whom I am now the sole guardian and support. Since I am to return Home at any time I want to make arrangements for my child to return also. Service regulations do not appear to permit my child to travel with me, therefore I am forced to make private arrangements.
>
> The child is Eurasian by birth, and Anglo-Indian to be precise. You have better know this now as I feel it may influence your decision. He is however, pale skinned and speaks and behaves like any ordinary kiddy. He is living with an English family in Shillong Assam, who are friends of mine. I

can assure you that this little fellow is well worth any trouble expended upon him.

I feel that a lady would be more suitable for the position of escort to the little chap, as he has a great deal of respect for the feelings of women. He is more or less capable of looking after himself in little ways so that all the escort would need to do during the voyage would be to see that he does not fall over the rail and takes time off from playing to go to his meals.

I am prepared to pay the cost of the full fare (£70) of his escort providing she will carry out the following:

1. That she will make an application to the Civil Controller of Passages for passages for herself and the child naming herself as the child's guardian during the voyage. When I made an application for a priority for him the authorities demanded the name of his escort. I was therefore unable to make those arrangements. His priority should be in Group B no. 6, which I am told is a pretty reasonable priority.

2. I want the escort to make the necessary arrangements with the Travel Agency for tickets etc. Here again, I shall not be in the country so I should find it well nigh impossible to make arrangements myself.

3. I must have the assurance of some rendezvous with the escort in the U.K. so that I can collect my little ward as quickly as possible after he arrives in the country. I live in London, but I do not expect the escort to deliver him to my home, more especially, of course, if she lives in the North. I would leave the rendezvous to the convenience of the escort, perhaps her own home might be best?

I see by your letter that you have been a missionary in China. I had better tell you then that my little ward is a Roman Catholic. If that is not your own denomination and we decide upon an agreement, I must ask you not to attempt to interfere with the little chap's ideas, for I don't want his mind filled with jumbled ideas resulting in his not knowing what to believe! I expect you see my point, even though I may not have made it very clear!

The proposed date of sailing I would leave to you, the earlier the better of course. Also, I shall pay all passage money for the escort and child in advance. Any further expenses incurred by the child would be reimbursed upon the arrival in the U.K.

The child's passport is in order and arrangements for his reception at home are almost complete. It simply remains for some suitable lady to take him home for me at her own convenience. I do not anticipate any trouble from the little chap by way of behaviour, he is primarily a boy and acts like all boys. I expect he will be sea-sick like everybody else, although he has travelled by air and not been air-sick which is much the same. This will be his first sea trip for all time.

There is one very major snag that I can see and that occurs when you are finally called for the boat. This child lives in Shillong, as I said before and it will take time to get him to you. I am told that only 10 days notice of sailing is given so that every moment would count in getting to the docks. To overcome this would you be prepared to have the child come to you some short time before you think you are due to leave, and then you could get away on time? I think I can arrange to have him delivered to you. I can see very obvious snags to this but I cannot see the obvious way out.

If my proposals are of interest to you I would be extremely obliged by an immediate reply as time is getting short and I want to fix this thing up before I leave the country. Trusting you will give this your consideration, I remain,

Yours truly,

Nelson Taylor

On 17th October, Miss Mabert penned her reply to Nelson. She assured him that she would be more than capable of being my guardian on the voyage from India to England, and she began to make preparations for what would become the last leg of this rescue mission. (Original letter on pages 194-197.)

Dear Mr. Taylor,

I am in receipt of your letter of the 11th Instant regarding the care of your ward you desire accompanied to the U.K. and have noted the principal points contained therein.

I am approaching the Authorities through Messrs. Cox & Kings (agents) Ltd., Calcutta, who are my agents, for an early sea passage for myself as escort for your ward.

I regret that as I am living in a Y.W.C.A. it will not be possible to have your ward with me but some very reliable friends of mine have agreed to accommodate him at a charge of 5 rupees per day if under 10 years of age and 7 rupees per day if over.

In the meantime would you please see that the boy is in possession of an up to date passport, vaccination and inoculation for Cholera certificate.

With regard to a meeting place on arrival in Britain, I shall cable you as soon as I know the date and port we shall disembark at, and it would facilitate matters if you could arrange to meet either the steamer or the train by which we shall be travelling.

It would be advisable if you kept in touch with Messers. Cox & Kings (agents) Ltd. Kings House, 10 Haymarket, London, S.W. 1 who will be fully informed of my movements.

I note your remarks in regard to funds for payment of our passages etc. and would advise you that the money may be paid either to my Bankers – Floyd's Bank Ltd, 37 Chowringhee, Calcutta or Cox & Kings (agents) Ltd., 5 Bankshall Street, Calcutta.

I would like to add that I am a music mistress by profession and have had ample experience in dealing with children. You can rest assured that your ward will receive every care and attention.

Yours truly,

Kathleen Mabert

P.S.

With my application for passages I have enclosed a copy of your letter to me so that the Civil Passage Controller – New Delhi will be fully informed of the position.

K.M.

This was the final letter that Nelson received in India. Soon after, he was demobilized, and he boarded a ship home to England. Days before he departed the country, he wrote to tell me that he was being discharged, and that he would not be able to bring me home to England himself. Instead, I should travel to Calcutta to meet up with a missionary lady who would accompany me on my journey home. My foster family read me this letter and explained Nelson's plan. The father would travel with me to Calcutta and ensure that I entered into Miss Mabert's care. I was gripped with anxiety. What would happen if the missionary lady wasn't there when we arrived? How would I contact Nelson if something went wrong? There were only a few moves left in this game of chess, and I could afford no mistakes. My very life depended on all the pieces lining up in just the right order. Luckily, Nelson's plan was well thought out. My voyage to Calcutta went off without a hitch.

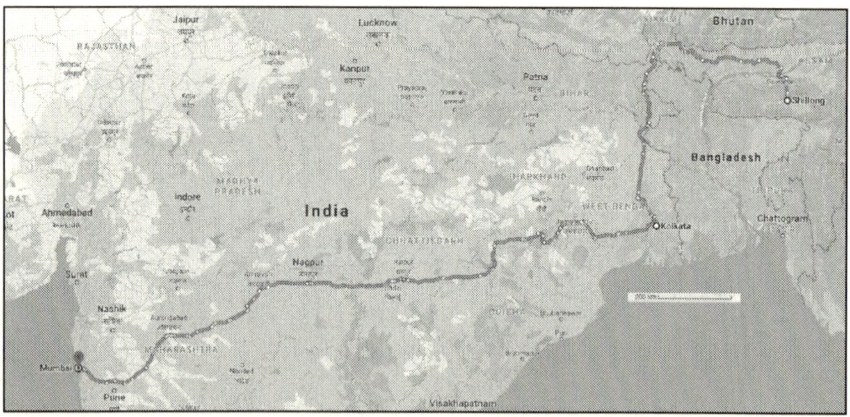

This would be the penultimate leg of my five-year Indian odyssey. Starting in Shillong, I travelled south to Calcutta and then took the train across the country to Bombay.

I said farewell to Jane and my foster mother and packed my few belongings into an old trunk that Nelson must have given me. I still have that trunk to this day. It is the only item that I still possess from my former life in India. I travelled with my foster father nearly 1,200 kilometres from Shillong to Calcutta to stay with Miss Mabert's associates there. Miss Mabert met me at the train station and explained that we would soon be leaving for our trip across the country. Together, we would trek more than 2,000 kilometres southwest by train to Bombay, where our ship awaited us.

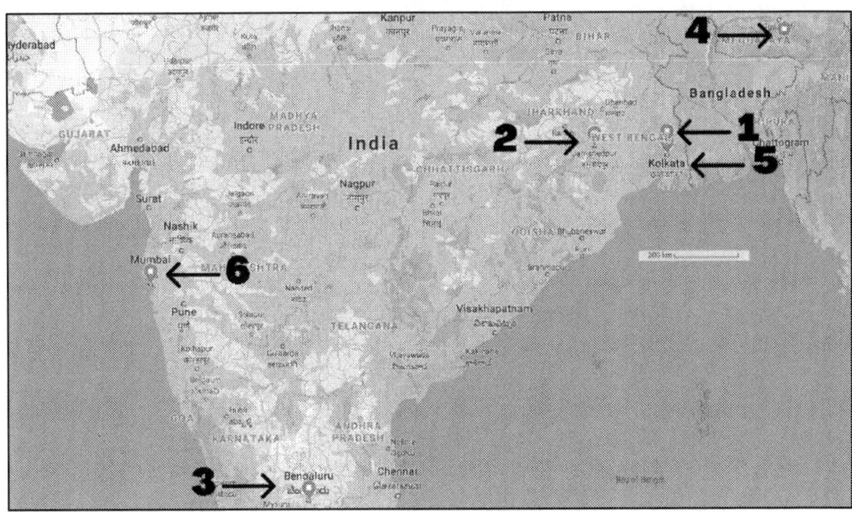

This map encompasses my full itinerary across the length and breadth of India. 1: Chandannagar. 2: Jamshedpur. 3: Bangalore. 4: Shillong. 5: Calcutta. 6: Bombay.

On 31st October, Miss Mabert received the confirmation that we had all been hoping and praying for ever since Nelson had decided he was going to adopt me nine months earlier. I had been granted passage into England. (Original letter on page 198.)

Please note that the priority under Category VI-c Serial Number 330N allotted to Miss K. Mabert has been upgraded to Category VI B Serial Number 164N. Please include Master Joseph Miller (aged 9) under this priority, as Miss Mabert has been nominated as his guardian.

Stu Spencer

Civil Passage Controller

My old chest trunk carried my few belongings from India to my new life in England.

The Civil Passage Controller permitted Miss Mabert and me to depart from the Port of Bombay in November. The journey would be more than 7,000 nautical miles and would take longer than a month, which would mean we would arrive in England around Christmastime, 1945.

As the ship set sail, I stood next to Miss Mabert, watching the land of my birth recede into the distance. After trekking the length and breadth of India on foot and by train, crisscrossing the country several times over, I felt that travelling halfway round the world in a boat would be a comparatively fun adventure. I knew that this was going to be the beginning of an exciting new chapter of my life.

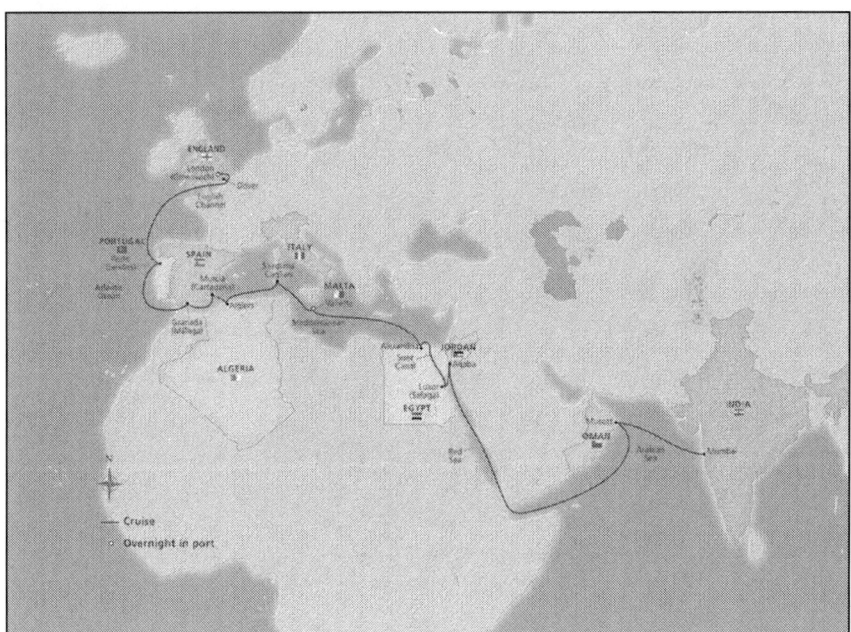

This modern-day cruise route uses the same itinerary as my passage from India to England. My 7,000 nautical mile voyage across the sea marked the end of my long Indian odyssey and the beginning of my new life in London.

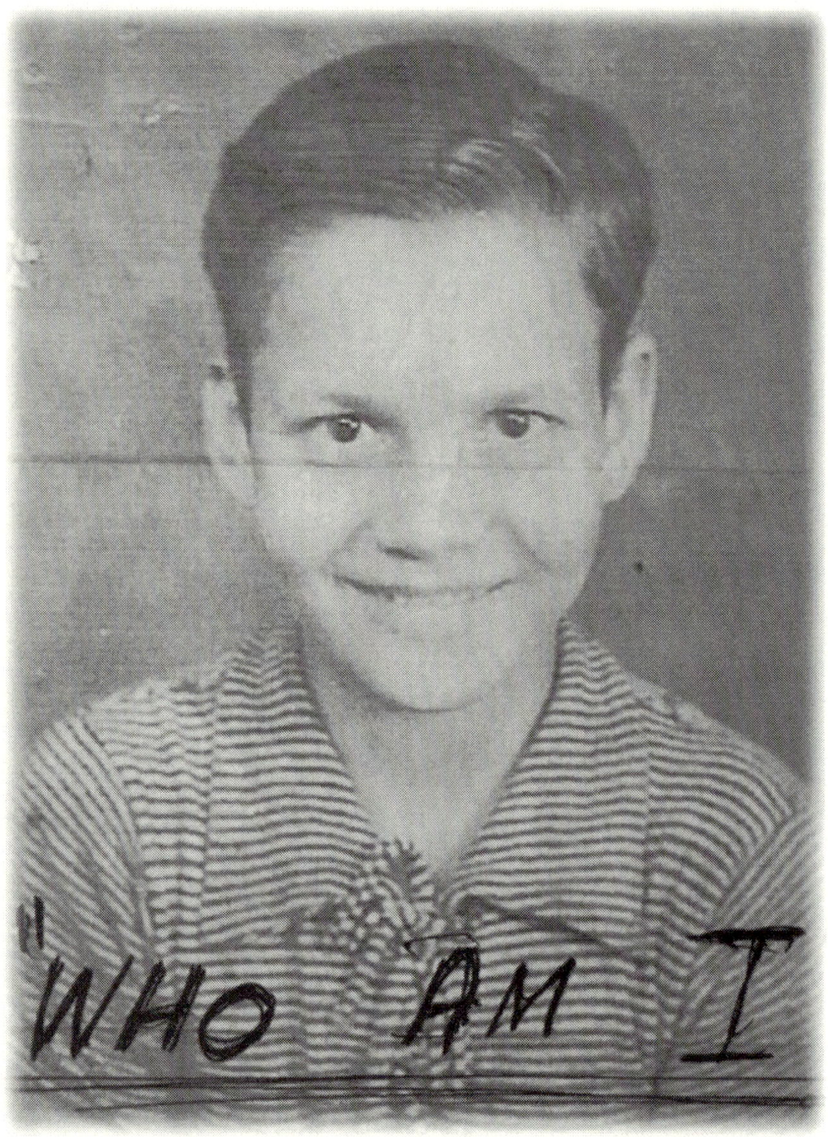

This is my passport photo from 1945 when my age was listed as ten years old. Many years later, I took a pen and inscribed on the photo the most elemental question that there is: "Who am I?"

CHAPTER 7

I don't recall much of my journey to England, except that it was long, and I had plenty of time to roam throughout the ship and play with the other children on board. I didn't do any schooling, which was fine by me. I spent my days getting up to mischief with the other kids my age. We played games of chase and hide-and-seek, running through the corridors and camouflaging ourselves within the maze-like architecture of the vessel. Another thing I remember was eating well. I'd had less than a year of regular meals, and my survivor's mentality was always seeking out my next source of food.

Miss Mabert the missionary lady kept watch over me as best she could. Her main job was to ensure that I slept in my bed and that I didn't fall overboard. To this end, she performed her work admirably. Nelson had paid for her passage to England in exchange for her guardianship, and once she delivered me to London, she would be able to complete her Christian mission and return to her home in Scotland.

This is the only photo I can find of Nelson. It was taken many years later at my wedding. The poor man never recovered his health after being a POW.

After more than a month at sea, I saw the White Cliffs of Dover for the first time. Our ship arrived at Southampton Docks on 26th December 1945. I had come to the end of a long, long road that had brought me from India to the start of a brand-new life. Miss Mabert accompanied me as we disembarked. Lo and behold, no sooner were we on dry land than I spotted Nelson and his father Albert waiting to greet me. A huge grin spread across my face when I saw Nelson standing there, and I could barely contain my joy. I rushed over to him as fast as my little legs would carry me. It was a huge relief to see him again. In the back of my mind, I had been fretting about what would happen if he weren't there to meet me. What would I do if I once again had to fend for myself on the streets, but this time in a foreign land where I still struggled to speak the language? But I needn't have worried, for there was Nelson, waiting with open arms.

I can still remember our journey from the docks to Grandfather Albert's house. The Taylors lived in a neighbourhood of South London called Tooting. From the Port of Southampton, we boarded a train and travelled 80 miles inland to London. This part of the journey felt familiar, although I was surprised by the velocity of the train. British trains moved considerably faster than the Indian trains I had ridden throughout my childhood. There would be no way I could clamber atop these steam engines and hope to catch a lift. The speed of the train would throw me to the ground. Once we arrived in London, we walked to the Underground station. I had never ridden a train underground before. I remember that I was fascinated by the sliding doors. They seemed to open and shut as if by magic.

Portrait of Albert Taylor during World War I, circa 1914.

Grandfather Albert was a great teaser, and he must have noticed the look of puzzlement on my face. Every time the door opened, he would nudge me to look closer at it. I was amazed that the door was simply opening on its own. As the journey went on, he nudged me again and this time nodded his head toward the back of the train. I turned to look, and there at the rear of the car stood a guard who held a lever in his hand. The next time the train stopped, he pulled the lever, and presto, the doors opened. My eyes went wide for a moment, and then I burst out laughing. The doors weren't magic after all, just very cleverly designed.

At last, we arrived at 120 Topsham Road, the Taylors' house and my new home. It was a small, city-owned rowhouse for which Albert paid rent. By now it was nighttime, and the lights were glowing warmly inside. It was Boxing Day, the day after Christmas, and what a Christmas present this was! For the first time in my life, a real family awaited me. Grandfather Albert opened the door, and I remember looking down a long hallway that stretched from the front door all the way to the back of the house. Then a woman's silhouette appeared in the hall. It was Nelson's mum, Nora. She waved to us, welcoming us inside. She took a look at me, standing there on the doorstep, and I'll never forget the first words out of her mouth. "Oh my," she said. "Why, you're dirty, and you look half starved!" Then she smiled and beckoned me through the door. "Come inside, dearie. You can call me Nan."

For the first time in my life, I felt truly welcome. It had been a risk coming here to live with the Taylors, far from the streets of India where I had learned how to survive. For all I knew, Nan could have been another Mrs. Miller, but she was good as gold. I remember feeling that a weight had been lifted off my shoulders. For so long, I had spent my days running from street to street, evading capture, and just trying not to starve. Then suddenly, here I was, crossing the threshold into this safe haven that was filled with love and warmth.

Portrait of Nora Taylor during World War I, circa 1914.

Nan told me, "The first thing we have to do is get you a bath." Nelson nodded and walked me up the stairs to the washroom where he drew a bath for me. He poured soap flakes into the water, which gave off a pleasing aroma. I remember soaking for a good long while. The hot water felt lovely after my journey at sea. When I had finished my bath, Nelson brought me a towel, and I dried myself. Then he presented me with some bedclothes. The fabric was crisp and fresh, and it felt soft against my skin. It was the first time I had ever worn something of this quality. When I was in India, I didn't wear anything on my feet, so I remember putting on the socks and slippers that were part of my outfit and thinking, "How on earth am I going to walk in these?" I must have looked like a puppy learning to walk in booties for the first time. I took large, gangly strides and tried to keep from tripping.

Once I was dressed and dry, Nelson led me downstairs to the dining room. Nan had set the table for dinner, and Nelson showed me where I was to sit. Nan placed some food on my plate, and I scarfed it down with my bare hands. In India, it is common to eat with the right hand, and I hadn't yet mastered the knife and fork. I must have been quite a sight for these upstanding British citizens, but if they thought my behaviour was crude, they didn't say anything. They knew I would learn proper etiquette in time. For I was now a British citizen, too. In India, I had been nothing, but here in England, I was an official subject of the Crown.

The food was delicious, and when I had finished my portion, I started licking my plate. Nan asked me if I would like some more, and

I hungrily said, "Yes, please!" I was still famished. After a childhood of surviving on scraps, this home cooked meal tasted like fine dining.

After I had finally eaten my fill, Nelson presented me with a gift. It was a little box done up in wrapping paper, tied round with a string that was looped in a bow at the top. I had never received a gift like this in my life. At Nelson's prompting, I untied the string and tore off the pretty paper. I opened the box, and inside I saw a toy car. I gasped and grabbed the little car in my hands. It was a bluish-green scale model with a tiny steering wheel and little seats inside. Nelson pointed to a winding key on the side of the car and indicated that I should turn it. I cranked the key a few times, and then Nelson told me to place the car on the ground. As soon as the wheels touched the wooden floor, the little car zipped across the room and crashed into the wall. I laughed with delight and chased after the tiny vehicle, utterly enthralled with my first real toy.

The Taylors gave me a Tri-Ang wind-up car like this to welcome me home.

After a few more zooms, I remember my delight transformed into fixated curiosity. I wanted to know what made this car run. There was a little opening in the bottom, and I could see gears and springs. Albert looked on approvingly. He was an engineer, and he could see by my fascination with this mechanical system that I had the makings of an engineer, too.

The toy came from my Auntie Doll. She was one of Nan's sisters, and she worked at the Tri-Ang Toy Factory in London. She loved to give me gifts, and every time she would come to visit, she would bring me a new toy car. Doll lived in the country with her sisters, Daisy and Doris. Nelson used to call them The Three Ds. Several months after I had gotten settled, Nelson arranged for me to visit my Aunties for the first time. They lived on an orchard, which was lined with rows upon rows of fruit trees with a bountiful crop hanging heavy from their branches. There were apples, plums, pears, and some fruits that I didn't recognize. When I arrived, I must have looked wide-eyed with wonder. My Auntie Daisy told me that I was allowed to go and play in the yard. I remember running eagerly throughout the wide acreage. I can still recall my first time picking an apple off of a tree. My Auntie Daisy called it a coxshire's apple. It was crisp, sweet, and delicious. When I came into the house later that afternoon for tea, I noticed a large bowl filled with apples in the middle of the table. Auntie Doris told me to help myself to an apple. I picked up the bowl to bring it closer to myself, and a melody started to play. I was mesmerized. It was a musical fruit bowl. I was amazed that such a thing could exist. That was just one of many visits to my Aunties. They spoiled me rotten and introduced me proudly to all their neighbours.

In addition to Nelson, Albert and Nora had an older daughter named Joan. Before I arrived in England, Joan had moved out of the house and had married an American bomber pilot named John Secord. He had flown a B-29 Superfortress during the War. Soon after, she became pregnant with her first son, Richard, and when he was born, she and John decided to move to the States to raise their family. Once they started their new life in America, we didn't see them very often. Another son, Rodger, and a daughter, Darlene, soon followed. Sadly, John Secord later took his own life. He couldn't forgive himself for the bombs he had dropped, the lives he had ended, and the families who would never see their loved ones again. The world didn't yet understand the way that post-traumatic stress slowly and insidiously eats away at the soldiers who return home. The War was over, and yet it was still killing the men who had offered their lives to the cause.

Nora and Albert had had another son, too, named John. John was the youngest of the three children, and when he was seventeen, the War broke out. He begged Albert to sign the papers that would give him permission to enlist. Even though he was a year too young, he still wanted to fight for his country. When I arrived at Topsham Road, there was a photo of John in his naval uniform on the mantle. I had already met most of the family, so I asked Nan who this young man was. She explained that John had been killed in battle when his ship was torpedoed by German submarines. As she stared at the picture of her son, her eyes welled with tears. She glanced at me, and then turned her gaze back to the photo. I looked closer, and I could see a certain resemblance between myself and this young man. I think in Nan's eyes, I filled a little bit of the void that had been torn into the fabric of her family when John died. Albert was never the same man after having to bury his son. I don't think he ever forgave himself for signing those papers that allowed John to join the Navy. He lived with that guilt for the rest of his life.

Most of what I knew about the War came from seeing newsreels. Growing up in India, I hadn't experienced the utter devastation of the guns, tanks, and bombs that had ripped much of the world asunder. When I came to London, I was shocked to see so many houses and buildings lying in ruins. Many people were homeless and were living on the streets. It reminded me of India in that way. The city put up makeshift shelters for people whose homes had been destroyed by the German bombing raids. These shelters would feed you and give you a place to wash, but not much else.

London didn't take long to recover itself. It soon started to rebuild. However, instead of building new houses, the city put up apartment blocks. They packed people into these units like sardines and charged them higher rates for the privilege. Work was scarce, and many people returning from the War couldn't get jobs, so it was difficult to afford this new housing. Some people tried living in these apartments, but they soon became overwhelmed by sharing such close quarters with strangers. Londoners were used to living in row houses, not in units stacked up high like boxes. Many of those who had family in other parts of England left London, abandoning their apartments, and the city was forced to condemn a number of these buildings.

London children look at their destroyed home after a German bombing raid.

Life was difficult in those days after the War. Back in India, we ate better food than many of the civilians did in England. The UK was tightly rationed in those days. If you wanted to buy anything, you had to get a ration book. You could only get a pound of this and half a pound of that. Meat and sugar were in especially short supply. It wasn't like it is nowadays, when you can go to the supermarket and load up with cartfuls of food. It was tough, but we survived. We always managed to have food on the table.

No matter how austere life in post-War London might have been, to me it felt like the lap of luxury. As far as I was concerned, I had gone from rags to riches. I basked in the Taylors' warmth and kindness, and I flourished from their generosity. My existence before had been precarious and chaotic. I lived day to day, barely surviving. My only concerns had been scrounging for food and finding safe places to sleep. Now thanks to the Taylors' love and care, I was transforming from a street kid into an upstanding young man. I remember that Nan would take me to the market with her and ask me to fetch groceries for her cart. I was eager to please, and I would bring her whatever she requested. I worked hard to show her that I was a good lad, and in turn she gave me her trust.

The Taylors were pleased with how quickly I was acclimating to my new life. As I began to venture out more often into the community, Nelson introduced me to the neighbours and made sure that I was treated with respect. People were curious, of course. It was clear that I was not related to anyone in the family. Nelson wanted to make sure that no one made any assumptions about me, so he shared my extraordinary story with people he met in the neighbourhood. Nelson was my protector, and thanks to him, I never experienced any discrimination. On the contrary, when people learned about my origins, they treated me with amazement and admiration.

Our next-door neighbour was particularly kind to me. Her name was Mrs. Stone, and she and her family were generous and friendly people. I remember one Saturday afternoon, I heard a tapping on the kitchen wall that divided our rowhouse from hers. I went outside to see who was knocking, and Mrs. Stone was standing there, smiling at me. She reached out and placed a few shillings in my hand. I looked at the money, and then looked up at her in disbelief. She smiled again and indicated that I should keep it. Then she went back inside. I thought, how wonderful! It was enough money to buy some candy or a small toy. But then I thought, what if I was wrong to accept this gift? I ran to Nan, and I told her what had happened. I asked her, "Is it okay to take Mrs. Stone's money?" Nan said, "I don't think there's any harm in it. If you feel guilty, you can give it back." I said, "Well no, Mrs. Stone said that I can have it." So, I kept the money, and the following Saturday, I once again heard Mrs. Stone knocking on our kitchen wall to give me a few shillings. It became our routine for a few months. This pocket money gave me a certain amount of independence, and it was not something I could ask of the Taylors; they had given me so much already. I couldn't thank Mrs. Stone enough. She was almost as good to me as Nan was.

I felt overwhelmed that so many people had reached out to me with such selfless generosity in their hearts. I could see how much the Taylors had sacrificed to adopt me. They were not destitute, but they were by no means wealthy, either. Yet here they were, pooling their limited resources to give me the gift of a happy childhood. They must have spent a small fortune to get me over from India. There was a list of people as long as your arm who wanted to immigrate to England after the War, and yet the Taylors and their friends like Uncle Leslie Brooks had called in all their favours to get me to the front of the line.

I realized that I could never repay the Taylors for saving my life. I remember I said that to Nan one day. I told her, "I shall never be able to pay you back for what you've done for me." She smiled at me and said, "You don't have to, love. You have paid us back with how far you have advanced. You have paid us back by being a good lad, and a good son." I knew that they had taken a chance on me. I could have turned out to be a real rascal. But I was a good boy, and I did as I was told. I wanted to prove to them that they had made the right choice in rescuing me, and I wanted to show them how grateful I was for this second chance at life. I made a promise to myself that I would do anything it took to make them proud.

CHAPTER 8

In early 1946, Grandfather Albert arranged for me to attend primary school for the spring term. According to my passport, I was about ten and a half years old. Although I was in truth closer to thirteen and a half, my small, thin frame would allow me to fit in with the younger children so I could brush up on my subjects before entering secondary school. I was able to speak enough English to communicate my needs; however, I found it frustrating that English was the only language that was spoken. I was used to the linguistic diversity of India, where everyone had to be proficient in many different tongues.

Albert enrolled me at Franciscan Primary School. School was a puzzling experience for me at first. It was enough of a cultural shock to be living in an unfamiliar country filled with foreign people and odd customs. I now had the added challenge of learning to fit in with my peers. It felt quite bewildering to be dropped into a classroom with forty strange children and be expected to get along with them. London at that time was nothing like London today. All the other boys and girls were white, and my tan complexion, curly brown hair, and dark brown eyes made me a curiosity to them. I don't remember making friends with any of my classmates that year.

It had been several months since I had attended St. Edmund's College in Shillong. I had lost what little ability I had acquired to read and write in English, and I struggled with my other subjects, too. Although English was the only language I had ever formally studied, my formative years spent as an illiterate orphan meant that learning any written system was a challenge. The spring term at Franciscan Primary School went by in an overwhelming blur. I was terrified of doing poorly in school. If I made a mistake, would the teacher beat me like Mrs. Miller did when I got in trouble? If I didn't do as well as Grandfather Albert expected of me, would the Taylors send me back to India? Fortunately, my primary school teachers were patient and kind, and they treated me with respect. I don't remember much of what they taught me; however, I must have done well enough to please Grandfather Albert. The school year ended, and Albert informed me that I would next be attending Hillbrook Secondary School for Boys.

Soon it was autumn of 1946, and I was considered to be eleven years of age. I entered Hillbrook on 9th September 1946, and that was where my schooling days truly began. I started at the bottom of my class, still grappling with the language barrier. I laboured to learn my subjects, and on more than one occasion, I had to fight back tears of frustration when I received low marks in a class. My first year at

Hillbrook was tough. I was mixing with boys who were twelve years old and who had started primary school when they were five, and here I was trying to cram nearly seven years of education into a one-year period.

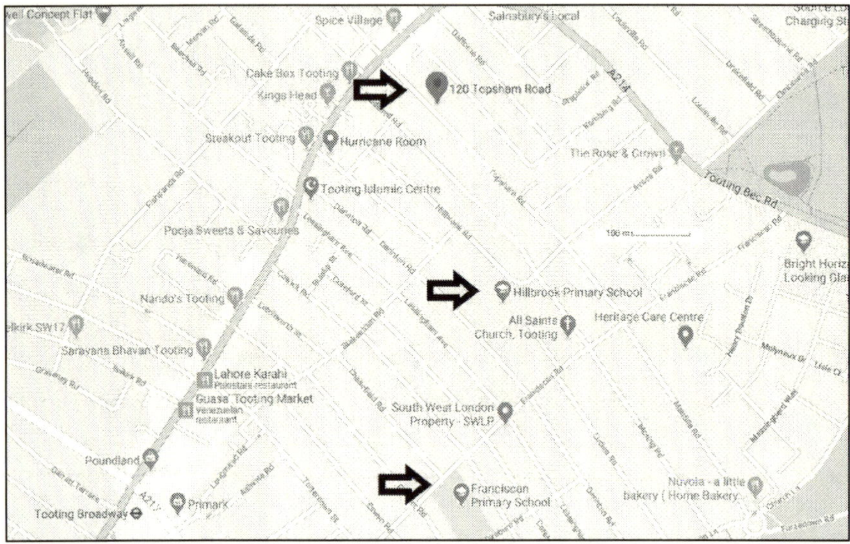

The location of the Taylors' house at 120 Topsham Road relative to Franciscan Primary School and Hillbrook Secondary School For Boys (which is now a primary school for girls and boys). I was used to travelling dozens of kilometres by train just to find my next meal. Now, my day-to-day life was contained within less than a one-kilometre stroll.

I was lucky to have some excellent teachers who were patient with me and dedicated to helping me succeed, even though I still struggled to read and write. My English teacher, Mr. Hayworth, realized that I needed more help than I would be able to receive in class, and he asked me to stay after school a few days each week so he could tutor me privately in reading, writing, and penmanship. I was grateful for his attention and help. Thanks to his coaching, I was able to receive passing grades in English my first year. He was a wonderful teacher.

The only problem with this arrangement was that it gave the Taylors some cause to worry about my behaviour in school. I remember Grandfather Albert confronted me on several occasions after I returned home late from Mr. Hayworth's tutoring sessions. He demanded to know why I was being held back after school and asked me sternly if I had misbehaved or gotten a detention. I explained, "No, a teacher at school is helping me to write and speak English." I could see that Albert was watching for me to slip up and put my foot in it, and I knew that I must be careful. He held the power of life and death for me, and I understood that I must do whatever he said to the letter.

There were numerous subjects that I was required to take at Hillbrook. In addition to English, I had classes in mathematics, science, history, art, woodworking, metalworking, and many others. Some subjects, like English and penmanship, were always a challenge. Others like science got easier over time. I excelled at metalworking, woodworking, and art. I loved my art class. I remember studying the architecture of Ancient Rome and drawing the columns and archways of the Forum and the Colosseum. My art teacher, Mr. Clifton, was a Frenchman, and he also taught my French class. French is a wonderful language, and I wish I had been able to give that subject more of my time and attention; however, it was all I could do to learn to speak and write proper English. Even though I remember the Hillbrook School fondly, it was an abrupt shift for me. I had come from India speaking

Hindi and other dialects, and then suddenly I was expected to forget the languages of my childhood and learn only English and French.

Many of my grades were understandably low my first year at Hillbrook. On my report card in June 1947, I received a D in Composition, a C in Spelling, and a D in Reading. Mr. Hayworth did recognize that I was "improving." In Scripture, I received a B, which was one of my better grades that year. Mr. Clifton gave me a C+ in French and wrote that I was "keen." In Mathematics and Geometry, I received a D and a C, respectively. In History, I received my lowest grade, an E, though in Geography, I received a C. I did better in Science and Art and received a B and a B-. Woodworking was my best subject and was the only class in which I received an A. My conduct was described as "good" and my attendance "satisfactory." The General Report states, "Joseph is very keen but at times is inclined to let his tongue run away with him." This makes me chuckle. Apparently, I was starting to come out of my shell. My report card was signed by Headmaster Gosling, a short, tubby man who would become a champion of mine in the years to come. (Original report card on page 199.)

The Taylors were all leaders of the Sea Cadets, which is an organization that trains children for service in the Royal Navy, and as a member of the Taylor household, I was expected to join. Grandfather Albert enrolled me when I was eleven according to my passport, and I stayed with the organization until I was discharged at eighteen. Luckily, I enjoyed my time with the Sea Cadets because I didn't have much choice in becoming a member. Albert was the commanding officer, Nelson was the second in command, and Nan was the captain of the girls' unit.

This photo was taken the first year I was with the Sea Cadets in 1947. That summer, my Sea Cadet football team played at Wembley Stadium, which was a great honour. I am the little boy in the front row. The youngest player on the team was named team mascot, so at 11 years old, that role went to me.

Nelson introduced me to the other children and made sure that everyone knew that I was his son. Since Albert, Nelson, and Nan helped run the organization, the children treated me with respect. To my surprise, I quickly made friends with the boys and girls in my level. These were the first children my age that I had ever truly counted as mates. There was no possibility for friendships while I was living on the streets of India. The last time I had been friendly with my peers was at St. Joseph's orphanage when I was six years old. I was grateful to the Taylors for creating a smooth transition for me so that I never felt out of place. I was able to jump in with both feet on the ground.

The Sea Cadets trained us in military drills to prepare us for service in the Royal Navy. In this photo, I am the small lad in the front row, fourth from the right.

Many of my friends in the Sea Cadets also went to Hillbrook, which meant that I never had to worry about bullies at school. My friends would always back me up. I was a newcomer from another country, yet they accepted me with open arms. They were interested in my story and where I came from. This core group of friends helped make my secondary school years one of the happiest periods of my life.

I learned valuable lessons in teamwork during my years with the Sea Cadets. The drills taught us to work together toward a common goal.

The Sea Cadets were like a junior Navy. We wore Naval uniforms, we practiced drills, and we learned how to use Naval equipment. It was preparation for joining the Royal Navy when we reached adulthood. It was a good program and was a lot of fun. When we were on school break, we would go to Training Ship Neptune, which was a Naval training facility on Raven's Ait Island on the River Thames. There we would practice rowing, sailing, and other skills that were required for being a Naval Officer. The island of Raven's Ait was set up like a summer camp. There were wooden buildings where we would sleep and eat our meals, and during the day we would learn everything from knot tying to navigation. It was a vacation that I looked forward to with great anticipation each year.

Life with the Taylors was active; there was never a dull moment. I always had something to do, even if it wasn't at home. If I finished my chores early, Nan would allow me to go outside and play. I would hurry through my duties, whether it was mowing the lawn, cutting the hedge, or doing the wash. Then I would go out with my friends. It sometimes seemed unfair that I had so many chores to do while my classmates were out playing; however, I later realized what a gift it was that Nan had taught me to be self-sufficient. I could cook, clean, operate machinery, and do many other household tasks. Nan had a tough life, and I enjoyed being able to help her around the house. One of our chores that I remember well was doing the weekly wash. They didn't have modern washing machines in 1940s London. We would labouriously roll the wash through an old mangle using a hand crank, and then we would hang the clothes on a line to dry. My friends were amazed at all the different types of housework that I was able to do, and I was surprised that they didn't know how to do things that seemed basic to me, like cooking a family meal. Looking back, I realize how much I learned from Nan. She was my guardian angel.

When the weather was nice, my friends and I would ride our bikes for hours through the London streets. The days just flew by. There was so much going on that I never had a dull moment. As I have grown older, I often hear kids say, "I'm bored." Well, they should have grown up in my day, when we didn't have cell phones, computers, or video games. We didn't even have calculators. All my calculations were done on a slide rule until I was well into adulthood. Time marches forward, but it is important to remember where we have been.

During my first summer of secondary school, Grandfather Albert arranged for me to get a paper route. He wanted me to have work experience, and I enjoyed having a few shillings in my pocket to spend how I pleased. The Taylors never gave me pocket money; they expected me to earn what I got, which helped me develop a determined work ethic. I knew from my years living on the streets that I didn't like handouts; it was always safer to do work and get paid.

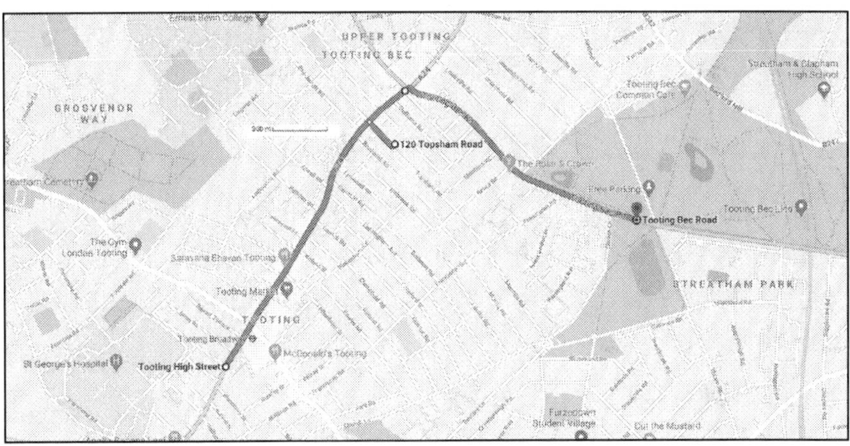

My paper route from my house at 120 Topsham Road to the intersecting Tooting High Street and Tooting Bec Road.

My paper route was fairly simple. It consisted of my street, Topsham Road, as well as the nearby Tooting High Street and Tooting Bec Road, which intersected a few blocks from my house. The paper shop was also a confectionery store. I would bike to the shop, get my newspapers, and then ride off to work. At the end of my route, I would pedal back to the shop and buy myself some sweets with my hard-earned money. This was the start of my working career.

The summer of 1947 flew by, and before I knew it, I was back at Hillbrook for my second year. Through my innate drive and Grandfather Albert's discipline, I pushed myself to achieve better marks and the recognition of my teachers. That year, Nelson too fulfilled one of his academic ambitions and became a teacher himself. He was a talented musician and played the piano beautifully, so it was a natural fit for him to become a music teacher.

It just so happened that Nelson's first teaching job was at the Franciscan Primary School where I had spent my first academic term in London. It was unfortunate that I left the school before he started teaching there. I would have loved to have taken music lessons with him, but it never came to pass.

Sometimes he would bring me in to speak to his class. He had about forty children in his classroom, and when he would introduce me, he would tell his pupils that I was his son. When he made this announcement, there would always be a few quizzical looks that would dart round the room because the children knew that Nelson was unmarried. How could this man have a son? Then Nelson would smile and explain, "Joey is my adopted son. We met while I was serving in the RAF in India, and I brought him to England with me after the War." Nelson seemed to enjoy introducing me this way. He liked to highlight the sheer improbability of my rescue and adoption into the Taylor family, as if sometimes even he still couldn't believe that it had all worked out so well.

CHAPTER 9

My third year at Hillbrook was when I really started to shine. I still struggled in my subjects, but my teachers acknowledged my efforts and reflected my hard work in their grades. In English Composition, I received a C for my exam but a B for effort in class. My English teacher that year commented on my report card that I was "making steady progress." Likewise, my History teacher gave me a C for my exam but a B for effort and wrote that I was "a good worker." In Mathematics, I received a D for my exam but a B for effort. I remember I tried very hard in that class. My Geography teacher graded my exam a C but my effort in class an A for "a good year's work." Science was a D this time, but my effort was a B, and my science teacher commented that my "teamwork is good." Biology was a pair of Cs and a statement that my work was "average." That was my lowest grade for effort that year. Art was a C with a B for effort, and the statement that, "He has done some good work." In Geometry, my teacher gave me an E on my exam but graded my effort a B, and he wrote that I had done "good work throughout the year." My music teacher did not give us an exam, but he awarded me a B for my overall work in class. My Woodworking teacher gave me an A for both my exam and my effort, and it was clear to both of us that I was a skilled craftsman. At the bottom of my report card, the Headmaster, Mr. Gosling, wrote, "He has done a good year's work. He works conscientiously, has made considerable progress. Takes an active interest in all school activities." My report card was signed by Headmaster Gosling and by Mr. Clifton, my favourite art teacher, who was my class master that year. Looking back, I realize how fortunate I was to have such good teachers who understood the challenges I was up against and acknowledged my hard work even when my exam scores were lower than those of my classmates. (Original report card on page 200.)

A few days after school started in September 1948, Headmaster Gosling asked me to be the Senior Prefect. There were nearly 450 boys in my school, so to be made a prefect was a great honour. It was my responsibility to organize the boys in the playground and the hallways, to keep them in line, and to make sure they didn't start fights. I had a lot of support from my friends at school who were my comrades in the Sea Cadets. We were sort of like a fraternity, and at school they were my helpers. I would give them duties to perform, and they would follow my orders. They were also my protectors, and they made sure that no one bullied me or gave me trouble. Looking back at it, I am genuinely surprised that no one ever laid a hand on me when I was at school. Here I was, an adopted half-Indian orphan from a world away, and they were all white and British, with family trees that could be traced back for generations.

I had a great friend in my class named Billy Head. Billy was a friend I had made in the Sea Cadets, and he was my bodyguard. He was as big as an ox, and whenever I needed him, he was right there, standing behind me, making sure that even the bigger lads respected me. Once I became Senior Prefect, Billy helped me sort out the squabbles at school and saw to it that no one tried to pick a fight with me. Along with Billy, I often hung out with Amos and Sanders. Sanders was a tremendous swimmer, and when he entered a pool, he just flew. The three of them were super friends. They were so helpful to me that after I became Senior Prefect, I asked Headmaster Gosling to make them my prefects. They were all bigger than me, and I needed their help to sort things out when some of the taller boys would get into fights. One of our main jobs was to keep the peace, especially when it was playtime and all the boys were in the yard. We would have to separate the brawlers, and if the fight was serious, we would take them to the Headmaster so he could discipline them. Billy, Amos, Sanders, and I had an awesome bond. They had all been curious about me when we first met in the Sea Cadets. My tan skin was still a novelty in a country where pale complexions were the norm. However, I don't think they ever viewed me with prejudice, just quiet interest.

Unfortunately, Albert didn't like most of my friends. I'm not sure why, but he especially disliked Billy. He told me one day, "Joey, you are not to associate with that boy." My friends were not allowed to come into the house. If I heard them walking up the road in the evening, I would sneak downstairs, trying my hardest not to make noise. Albert went to bed early, and he would get ever so upset if he were disturbed. I would slip out the front door and go out to meet them so they wouldn't ask to come inside. Of course, Albert couldn't do much to stop me from socializing with Billy and my other friends. At school, we were thick as thieves, and we were always together during Sea Cadet training.

Even with Grandfather Albert's strict regime at home, life as a teenager was exhilaratingly fun. At school, I was heavily involved in athletics. I loved running and swimming, and I played football and cricket. Cricket is my all-time favourite. The only sport I didn't play was rugby, which was too rough for my liking. Because of my involvement in the Sea Cadets, I was also an excellent rower.

After my third year at Hillbrook, Billy, Amos, Sanders, and I went to Training Ship Neptune for our summer holiday with the Sea Cadet Corps. That summer, my buddies and I competed in the rowing race. The boats we rowed were like Viking longships. They were nothing like the light rowing craft that you'll see in races between Oxford and Cambridge. They were heavy and made of wood with thick sides and large wooden oars. In each boat there were five boys, four to row and one to steer. I was the stroke and sat in the front of the boat. Billy sat behind me, followed by Amos and then Sanders. A fifth friend named Peter Pope sat at the rear and steered the boat. We all put our backs into it. We were bounding with muscles and even though we were still teenagers, we looked more like young men.

My mates and I in the Sea Cadets would train in all manner of military drills. In this photo, we were learning how to work together to move a heavy cart.

We had a ball living together on Raven's Ait Island. There were no parents telling you what to do, and even though there was discipline, my friends and I mostly did as we pleased. There were certain rules we had to obey, however, in order to get out on the water. We had to get up in time for breakfast, and we had to do our chores, but then we were free to go down to the boats. We would take food with us and spend all day on the river, practicing our rowing and having fun.

There were Sea Cadets from various areas of London who competed in the rowing race. It was sort of like the Olympics, except instead of coming from different countries, the teams came from different city districts. I think there were about six different crews.

There was a riverside crew that was heavily favoured to win the race. They lived in an area of London near the Thames, and they'd had more time to practice on the water than any of the inland crews.

The only way we could hope to beat them was by practicing, and boy did we practice. We were on the river for hours and hours each day, rowing back and forth. Sometimes the rival teams would stand on the river's edge and watch us to see if they could figure out what our strategy was because they could tell we were rowing full out with giant oar strokes. We would often laugh and row over to them and then speed away, just to needle them.

The other teams never did figure out our strategy. Grandfather Albert had designed special foot straps for us to use, similar to toe clips on a bicycle. These foot straps allowed us to angle our torsos all the way back without falling, which gave us a fuller stroke than any of the other teams. Anyone watching could see us leaning back with each stroke, almost as if we were reclining in the boat, but they never figured out how we kept from toppling backwards.

Grandfather's contraption gave us the edge we needed over the other teams. On the day of the race, we got an early lead, and we never lost it. We beat the other teams down the entire width of the river, and we won the race. I still have the medal somewhere. To this day, I can picture the expressions on the riversiders' faces when they realized they had just been beaten by a land team. The riversiders thought they were the kingpins, and by all rights, they should have won. They had more practice on the water, but they didn't have Grandfather Albert's engineering skills. In the end, I think they learned their lesson. Never be too confident because with a little ingenuity, another team can beat you.

It was exhausting work, mind you, winning that race. The oars were heavy, and we weren't allowed to wear gloves, so my hands were raw and covered with blisters. Achieving that victory alongside my best friends was the crowning glory of the summer. It was a proud moment, especially when we were all presented with our medals. I remember Albert was especially pleased with me when I got back home. I think he was glad to see that I had learned a lesson of engineering—all problems can be solved, but sometimes you have to think outside the box.

In the autumn of 1949, I returned to Hillbrook Secondary School for my fourth and final year. I was now considered to be fourteen years of age. At the start of the school year, the Headmaster, Mr. Madge, took me aside one day and asked me to become School Captain. This was an honour and a great responsibility, and I was stunned. I knew that I still struggled with many of my subjects, but I reasoned there must be something that the Headmaster saw in me that made him decide to elevate me to the highest student position. I had been chosen out of all the boys in my class to oversee the prefects and ensure that the students maintained order and discipline. I thanked Headmaster Madge and said that I would speak to my family about it. As soon as I returned home that afternoon, I told Nan and Albert the news.

I still remember Nan's face when I told her. I said, "Nan, I'm really scared. There's more than 400 boys there. But to think that out of all those boys, I was picked for School Captain, I must have done something good." She beamed at me and said, "Go for it, Joey. Do it. Take the opportunity." Nan was my guiding light. No matter what hesitations I had in life, she would always encourage me and tell me that I could do it. She was a wonderful lady.

The next day I went to school and told Headmaster Madge that I had talked with my family and I was happy to accept the position. He instated me right away. My duties were to advise the other boys when they had questions, control them when they got rowdy, and intervene if they got into a fight. I also had to assist in the lunchroom, make sure the boys were all lined up, and reprimand them if they misbehaved while getting their food.

I was terrified, mind you. There were 450 boys, which was a big school, especially in those days. Fortunately, I had Billy, Amos, and Sanders as my prefects again. The four of us effectively ran the school while the masters were in the teachers' room having a break or drinking their tea. Especially on the playground, it was up to us to step in if the boys started fighting. We would separate them, sort them out, and figure out what the disagreement was. If there was a problem, it was our job to take it to the Headmaster, and if it was severe enough, we would have to go to the Principal. I never let being School Captain go to my head. I wasn't mean to any of the boys, and I tried to be fair with them when I was breaking up fights. As always, Billy was my protector, and nobody tried to hurt me when he was around. If they challenged or harassed me as School Captain, Billy and I could take them to the Headmaster or the Principal, and they would be reprimanded.

In my final year, it was clear to both myself and my teachers that I had improved considerably over my four years at Hillbrook. That year, there were no exams, just grading. I received a trio of C- in English Composition, Spelling, and Grammar. My English teacher that year was Mr. Darrington. He wrote, "Works well and tries hard." He deemed my conduct and attendance to be satisfactory. Mr. Darrington was a bit of a taskmaster, and I chuckle as I remember that my friends and I used to call him Mr. Derriere. My History teacher gave me a B, and in Geography, I received a C+. In Science and Biology, I received a pair of Bs, and my Algebra teacher gave me a C. In Metalworking and Woodworking, I received a pair of A-, and my teachers wrote that I was a "keen and careful worker" and "a good worker." Mr. Clifton, my art teacher, gave me an A- and wrote that I was "an extremely hard worker, has done some excellent work." I loved that class. I remember spending hours drawing freehand architectural designs of Roman buildings with a fountain pen and then colouring them in. I've kept my old art notebook to this day; it is rather tattered, but it still holds a place in my heart. Finally, Mr. Gray, my drafting teacher, gave me a B in Machine Drawing, and wrote "very good work done." Mr. Gray was one of my favourite teachers, and I had little idea how important his drafting class would become in only a few months' time. (Original report card on page 201.)

After school, my friends and I would go for long bike rides together. More often than not, our itineraries would lead us to the nearby girls' academy, which was Hillbrook's sister school. We would sneak onto the grounds and try to flirt with our female counterparts.

We were immature and a bit foolish. The teachers from both schools reprimanded us many times and told us not to go near the girls' school, but that just gave us more determination to talk to the young ladies. In fact, that was where I met my first girlfriend. Her name was Connie Parker, and we dated for about four years. I got to know her and her family quite well in that time. Her mum and dad were kind people and were good to me. Her dad was in the upholstery business. I remember watching as he would repair chairs and sofas. He would put a handful of tacks in his mouth, and one by one he would hammer them into the fabric. It seemed quite dangerous to me, though not as dangerous as Connie's grandfather, who worked as a window cleaner. He'd had numerous accidents in his life, and when I met him, his arm was in a brace. What I remember most about him was that he was an ace at playing checkers. He would always find a way to beat me. Mrs. Parker, Connie's mum, was like a second mother to me. She had a dark complexion like me, and people would often mistake me for her son. She would explain that no, I was her daughter's boyfriend, although I think she would have been happy to have me as a son-in-law.

Eventually, Connie and I drifted apart and then broke up, and after a while, she met another young man. The economy was bad in London at the time, and it was difficult to find work. After several years, they decided to move to Australia to start a new life and begin a family. Her grandfather passed away, and Mr. and Mrs. Parker moved to Australia to be with Connie and help her care for her four children. We remained friends for many years, and we used to correspond regularly, but eventually I lost touch with her and her family. I still think about them from time to time.

In the spring of 1950, I graduated from Hillbrook Secondary School. In England, the employment age started at fifteen, and children who had the skills and connections would enter the workforce. This started with a seven-year apprenticeship, and after that time, we would be allowed to pick a trade that we wanted to pursue. One day, my beloved art teacher, Mr. Clifton, pulled me aside and told me that he had a job for me if I wanted it. It was to work as a tombstone engraver for the headstones that went up on burial plots. I loved artwork and design, and I would have liked to have taken the job, but when I brought it up with Grandfather, he said no. He had already pulled some strings to get me an engineering apprenticeship at the London Electricity Board. Albert was a master carpenter there, and he happened to know the head of the engineering department.

I knew better than to argue with him. Albert was very strict. He was a tough disciplinarian, much more so than Nelson. Nelson was a good man, but he was often gone from the house and wasn't there to intercede on my behalf. Albert was the head of the family. When he said something, you did it, no questions asked, or there would be consequences. I felt sorry for Nan. She worked so hard, and he was often cruel toward her.

Albert had set up a seven-year apprenticeship for me, and after the seventh year, I was to become a draftsman. Albert chose that profession for me because I had shown aptitude in Mr. Gray's Machine Drawing class, and because being a draftsman was a profession befitting the Taylor household. With that, Albert shut down my dreams of being an artist. I couldn't argue with him. I was relieved to have a job lined up after graduation because a lot of my friends had no job prospects at all. England was still recovering from the War, and the economy was terrible. Some of my mates went on to become street children scrounging for odd jobs, not unlike the way I had lived my early years in India. I was one of the lucky boys to have a good job, especially with only five years of education under my belt. It was a blessing, but also a challenging experience to be expected to behave as an adult at the age of fifteen. I was to begin my apprenticeship that spring, and there was to be no more discussion on that.

It is sad, but I lost touch with Billy, Amos, and Sanders a few years after we all left school. We still saw each other in the Sea Cadets until we were discharged at age eighteen, but soon after that, we drifted apart. I'll always be thankful to those boys, and I'll never forget how they had my back whenever I needed it. They were my first true friends. In my life, there have been many kindred spirits who have gone out of their way to help me move forward along my path. I am eternally grateful to each and every one of them that welcomed me in, showed me kindness, and helped me succeed.

CHAPTER 10

As the summer of 1950 rolled around, I felt free as a bird. I was done with Secondary School, and for a little while at least, I wouldn't have to worry about teachers, books, or homework. At the same time, I was filled with nervous excitement for the beginning of my apprenticeship at the London Electricity Board. I was going to train to be a junior draftsman, which would give me a career path to become an engineer. I had been working in some capacity for much of my life. I had created little jobs for myself as a child to survive on the streets of India, and I had delivered newspapers to earn pocket money in the Taylors' home. This apprenticeship, however, would be my first real entrance into the workforce. I was quickly approaching adulthood, with all the liberties and responsibilities that it entailed.

I spent a summer of fun with the Sea Cadets at Training Ship Neptune, and as autumn approached, I said my goodbyes to my friends. It would be the first September in four years that I wouldn't get to pal around with my school chums and have their support and protection. I would once again be at the bottom of the pecking order. I knew that I would dearly miss the feeling of leadership that I had experienced as Senior Prefect and School Captain.

My final summer with the Sea Cadets was both happy and fraught with anticipation for what was to come. In this photo, I am the lad in the middle row, third from the right.

In late autumn, I began my apprenticeship. I was the youngest person in the workplace, which was quite intimidating. Many of the men who worked there were twice or three times my age with families of their own. Some of them had children who were as old as I was. At first, these men wanted little to do with me. My job consisted mainly of staying out of their way unless they ordered me to fetch them something that they needed. I had looked forward to doing actual drafting work with the drafting instruments that Grandfather Albert had bought me, and I was dismayed that my duties primarily entailed being a "goffer." I would "go for" this and "go for" that. All day long it was, "Joe, go do this. Joe, go bring me that."

The London Electricity Board headquarters at Cambridge Heath Road, Bethnal Green, London.

To make matters worse, the senior apprentices and junior employees would often play pranks on me. Many a time, someone would walk up to me and slap me on the shoulder to wish me "top of the morning" only to affix a sign on my back that read, "Kiss me!" They meant it all in good fun, but I was still a sensitive lad, and there were days when I nearly broke down crying. For the first few months, I would go home to Nan in a terrible state. She would reassure me, "Don't worry about it, dearie. It's just their way of accepting you." Still,

I was only a teenager, and it hurt having so many people picking on me day in and day out.

One morning, I remember one of the senior employees called me over to his bench. I must have looked especially down in the dumps because he said to me, "You know why they are picking on you, don't you?" I said, "No, I haven't the foggiest. I just wish they would stop." He said, "It's because they like you, Joe. Everyone in the workplace goes through this process. I went through it, and so did the rest of them. It's just the way we test each other's mettle. Before you know it, they'll stop teasing you, and you will all be the best of friends." I thought to myself, "He thinks they like me? That's the misunderstanding of the decade! If they like me, why are they treating me like a dog?" Still, I toughed it out, and as winter melted into spring, some of the more intense hazing dissipated as well.

Some of the employees picked on me not out of joviality but because of jealousy. Leslie Brooks was the senior draftsman in charge of the department, and he was the reason that I had gotten this apprenticeship. Up until that point, I had simply known him as Uncle Leslie. After he had helped the Taylors adopt me and bring me to England after the War, he had remained one of my biggest champions. He was invested in my success, and once I started working at the London Electricity Board, he became my mentor. Some of the other engineers were jealous of this. They wondered why I got all the attention from the boss.

After a while, I graduated from being a "goffer," and to my relief, I was allowed to start training as a draftsman. When I turned in my first work assignments, Uncle Leslie quickly realized that I was struggling with my penmanship. When I wrote, I still had difficulty with fine motor control, and I would form my letters up, down, and sideways. I couldn't write in a straight line to save my life, let alone do drafting at a professional level. Leslie took me under his wing. He was a hard taskmaster, but he was fair. He never gave me a critique that I didn't deserve, and I knew that he was tough on me because he believed in me. He taught me how to use a pen and ink properly and how to get all the letters to match up. He would draw a line, and then he would carefully write each letter along its length, creating a perfectly straight row of text. His words were evenly spaced, and each of his letters was the same height. I still remember trying it out after he had shown me the technique. I drew a line and used it as a guide, but even with this assistance, I found it challenging to print. Some of my letters were still too high or too low. I practiced every day, concentrating on making each of my words uniformly spaced. I made sure to always practice in ink because in drafting, we never used pencil. Eventually, I learned how to write my name in perfect balance. My letters were straight and all in a row.

I learned a lot from Uncle Leslie. He was part of the Taylors' extended family, and he was a father figure to me. He would often invite me over to his house for tea. I acquired my love of stamp collecting from him. He had many beautiful books of vintage stamps, and he showed me how to properly preserve my own stamp collection. I used to stick my stamps in a book willy-nilly, but Leslie showed me how to mount them properly. He used small, sticky, paper hinges and affixed one part to the stamp and the other part to the book. This prevented the stamps from becoming glued to the book itself. Whenever you wanted to move a stamp, you would simply peel off the sticky part of the paper. He also showed me how to use tweezers to handle each stamp. Up until that point, I had used my fingers, but this ran the risk of smudging or crimping the stamp's surface. The tweezers allowed me to gently lift up each stamp and keep it clean as a whistle.

As I was going through some old papers recently, I came upon Uncle Leslie's birth certificate. It says, "Leslie Brooks, born One Thousand Nine Hundred and Ten." I found it in a season's greetings card, and he may have sent it to me shortly before his death in the 1970s. I know that Uncle Leslie held a special place in his heart for me. In many ways, I was like his surrogate son. He had lost his first wife tragically in an accident, and afterwards his own son walked out of his life, abandoning the family until after Leslie's death when he returned to claim his inheritance. Leslie married again after his first wife died, and at first his new wife seemed like a nice lady, but she later became controlling and cruel. Many years after they were married, she turned on him and kicked him out of the house. He did a lot for her, and I think that her rejection truly broke him. He had a tragic life, and I am forever in his debt. He was one of my real champions, and he was such an important person in my story. If it hadn't been for Uncle Leslie, my adoption might not have gone through. He came to the Taylors' aid in their rescue mission, and he really did become my second father. I want to give him the recognition that he deserves for saving my life.

This photo was taken my first year apprenticing at the London Electricity Board. I am the lad second to the left. Leslie Brooks, my mentor and champion, is second to the right.

A few years into my apprenticeship, some of the guys in the office started treating me a bit better. I felt comfortable enough around a few of them to explain why Leslie Brooks had singled me out as his protégé. I remember that one of them asked me if I had ever been to Leslie's house, and I replied yes, I had been there many times for supper. Several of the guys who overheard me talking were jealous of this. You know how people can be when they know that someone is the teacher's favourite. However, I explained my past to them, and I told them that Leslie had been one of the people who had rescued me from India and made it possible for me to come to England. As they came to understand the precariousness of my past and Leslie's reason for favouring me, a few of the guys extended a hand of friendship to me. After that, several other men followed suit. Soon, I was palling around with a number of the guys in the office. We would go out together at lunch to walk and chat along the main street. Finally, going to work was no longer a chore. It took several years, but I had finally made some real friends. The London Electricity Board became a place where I felt welcomed and included, and I genuinely looked forward to being there each day.

The building where I worked used to be a tram depot. It resembled an old factory, with an open floor plan and high ceilings. I was told that when the trams had run in London years before, they were stored there at night. Many of the old tracks were still visible along the floor. The London Electricity Board took over the building after it became vacant. I remember looking up at the vaulted ceiling and seeing dust motes floating down from the ductwork, illuminated by the light that streamed in from the high windows. I worked at a drawing board, and I always had to cover my paper with a sheet before I left at night. The dust would gently rain down on us day in and day out, and I learned the hard way that if I didn't protect my desk, I would have a fine layer covering my work by morning. When I arrived at my bench each day, I would use a brush to sweep the dust off the top sheet before I rolled it back, and then I would get to work.

Now mind you, when I started my apprenticeship, I was still a young man with only four years of formal education under my belt, and I continued to struggle with many of my subjects. Reading and writing were still especially a challenge. They say that English is one of the hardest languages to learn, and that is true in my experience. It is a composite of so many other languages, and the pronunciation, spelling, and grammatical rules are incredibly unpredictable. You can say, "Where did the weary wayfarer cross the weir when he warily walked into the warehouse to wear his wares?" How ridiculous! And that is just one example. There are so many words that are pronounced similarly but have very different meanings.

I was lucky because soon after I began my apprenticeship, the London Electricity Board gave me one day off each week to go to technical college, and they also made it possible for me to take night classes. I decided that I would go for a degree in engineering. I attended the Wandsworth Technical College Day School and the Upper Tooting Junior Commercial and Junior Technical Evening Institute. Three nights a week, I would come home from work, eat a quick dinner, grab my bookbag, and ride off to class. It would often be dark by the time I returned home, and I would still have homework to complete before I went to bed.

These schools were very strict. If I got poor marks or missed class, they would report me to my employer, which would reflect badly on my job performance. The only acceptable absence was if I were sick, in which case I had to supply a doctor's note. This seldom happened because in those days, I was quite fit. I still struggled in my subjects, but I made sure to give them my best effort. I had learned from my days at the Hillbrook Secondary School that effort and drive count for a lot. (Original letters and reports on pages 202-204.)

At the Wandsworth Day School, I studied many different subjects, including mathematics, science, English, and history. There was always a lot of homework to do, which meant that I had even less time in my already busy schedule. I remember my chemistry homework was particularly difficult because I had to do the experiments over and over again until I got them right.

I preferred my evening classes, where I got to study drafting, metalwork, and woodwork. The Tooting Evening Institute had an engineering competition, and on the encouragement of one of my teachers, I submitted a drawing. It was a three-dimensional design of a roof structure, drawn in colour and with precise detail. I worked particularly hard on this piece, and my teacher was pleased with how it turned out. Shortly thereafter, I learned the good news—the judges gave me a 100% on my drawing, and they awarded me the top student engineering prize. I was overjoyed. For someone with relatively little education, I was progressing quickly.

Grandfather Albert was a carpenter, and funny enough, he taught an evening woodworking class at a rival institute. I remember one day, I happened to run into the principal of the night school where Albert worked. After we exchanged some pleasantries, he said, "You know, Joe, you walked away with a top student award. What are you doing at that school? We would be pleased to have you at our institute." I told him, "I'm studying woodworking, that's why I'm here." He said, "But why? Our woodworking class is better." I nodded and said, "Yes, but my grandfather is the instructor." He looked surprised, as many people did when they learned that I was part of the Taylor household. Today in London, it is commonplace for families to adopt children from other countries, but back then it was still a novelty.

I worked hard to prove myself. I wanted to show the Taylors, my teachers, my work colleagues, and everyone who helped me succeed that I was worthy of their investment. I made sure that I earned good marks in my subjects. I still have a report card from the Tooting Evening Institute, dated July 1952. At the time, I was taking English, Maths, Technical Drawing, and Workshop Practice. My teachers wrote that I was making excellent progress, and that my attendance was good. They also commented that I had a keen interest in the subjects that I was studying. This was true. I felt like a sponge, trying to soak up as much knowledge as I could. I knew that applying myself in school and earning my engineering degree would open the door to the next phase of my life—adulthood. (Original report card on page 205.)

According to my official papers, I turned eighteen on 15 August 1953. It was eighteen years to the day since my birth mother's friend had brought me to St. Joseph's Convent and entrusted my little life to Mother Superior Marie Agnes and her Sisters. I had few remaining memories from that time. Ever since Nelson had rescued me and brought me to England, I had tried to focus my mind forward on my studies, my work, and my life as a British subject. It was painful to think about those hungry years spent running throughout India, always on the brink of death. However, on my eighteenth birthday, Nelson presented me with a most unexpected gift. It was an exercise book, and as I looked upon it in curiosity, Nelson said, "Joe, this is your life." I didn't know what he meant, but as I opened the book, the pages turned to a collection of letters and documents from the end of the War. I gasped. Nelson was not exaggerating. Indeed, these precious pieces of paper marked the beginning of my new life.

As I paged through the documents, I read letters from Grandfather Albert and correspondence that Nelson had written. There were also many letters from people that I didn't recognize, all referencing my adoption by the Taylors. My heart pounded as I deciphered Father J. Comerford's nearly illegible scrawl and realized that he had asked some of his parishioners to search for me after I had run away from Mrs. Miller. I had tried to forget about that woman, and the memory of her cruelty was an unwelcome intrusion in my mind. Still, as I read about her, I felt vindicated in my decision to run, knowing that she had sent a search party after me.

I received another shock as I read Mother Marie Agnes' letters about me. For the first time in many years, I thought about my birth parents. I wished that I could remember the moment that my mother gave me away. I just wanted to know why. Did my mother's parents force her to give me up after I was born? Did my mother and father love each other, or was their union merely a brief affair? Did she ever think about me once she had entrusted me to her friend's care? Did she really die, or was that just a story to make it easier to place me in the orphanage? If she were still alive, did she miss me sometimes? And did my father return home to Scotland after the War, or was he killed serving his country? I desperately wanted to know what had happened to them. I had so many questions, and yet I knew that no matter how long I stared at these documents, I would not find the answers that I sought. These papers offered only tantalizing clues to my origins. And so, I used the stamp collecting skills that I had learned from Uncle Leslie to preserve the documents in an album where I could keep them safe. Then once again, I set my sights to the future and kept moving forward.

These are some of the letters and documents from India that Nelson saved for me. They are included in detail at the back of this book.

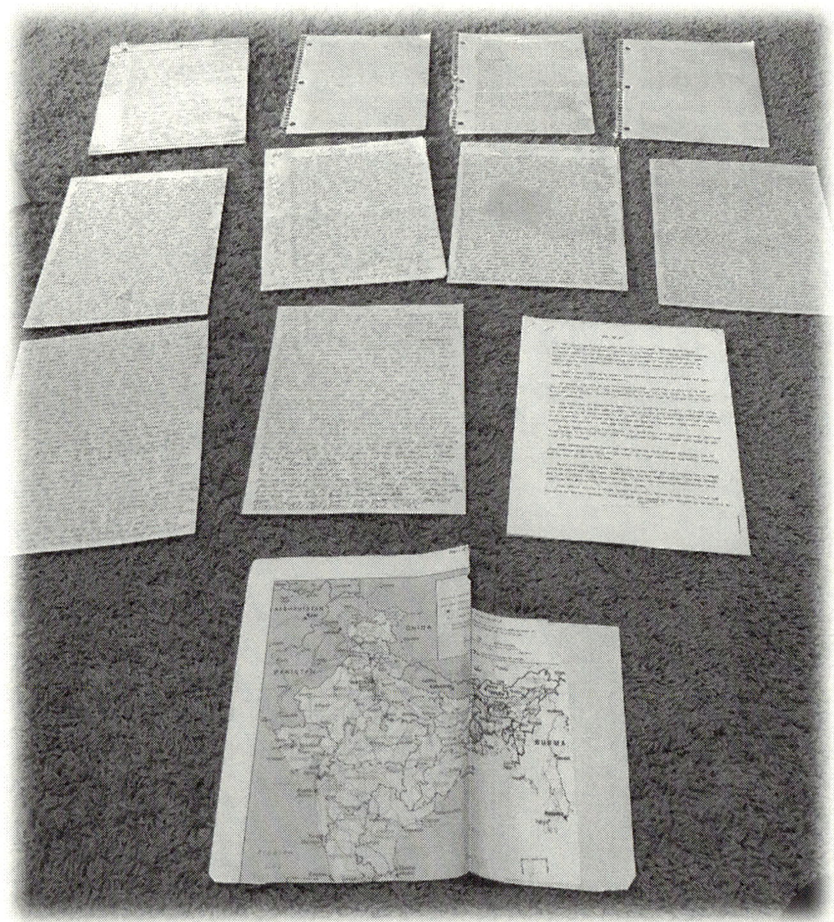

These are some of the letters and documents from India that Nelson saved for me. They are included in detail at the back of this book.

CHAPTER 11

My eighteenth birthday brought about many life transitions. For the past seven years, I had been a member of the Sea Cadets, and the program gave me structure as well as a friend group. Now that I was an adult, I was too old for their ranks. As soon as I aged out of the Sea Cadets, I enrolled in the Royal Navy Voluntary Reserve. It was further training to join the Navy, which is where I ultimately wanted to serve. Eighteen also brought about my first conscription notice. In England at the time, young men were drafted into the Army on their eighteenth birthday and were expected to complete two years of service. However, it so happened that I was in college sitting for my exams, and rather than forcing me to abandon my education, the Army sent me a letter informing me that they would waive my conscription until I had received my diploma. They instructed me that I was to report for service on or before my twenty-second birthday.

Here I am as a young man, posing for a formal picture. It is a far cry from that first photo I took for my passport all those years ago.

During my first few years at the London Electricity Board, I had ridden my bicycle to the office. I would get up early each morning and pedal for over an hour, no matter the weather. It was often rainy, especially in the winter, so to avoid looking like something that the cat dragged in, I would bring a change of clothes with me in my satchel. I would arrive, put on proper attire, and clock in before the workday began at 9:00 in the morning. Then I would work my shift until 5:00 p.m., taking a break for lunch, and I would ride my bike home at the end of the day. Bicycling to and from work became my routine, and I would have been quite content to continue, when in December of 1953, Albert and Nan gave me the gift of a brand-new motorbike to celebrate my eighteenth year. This motorbike gave me a newfound sense of freedom. It was a single seater with a 250cc engine, and all of a sudden, I was the envy of every boy my age. My new wheels made the trip to work much more pleasant and quite a bit faster.

The years flew by in my apprenticeship. My twenty-first birthday was one of the highlights of my life. I was now fully an adult, and I felt supported and accepted by the other men at work. It was a pleasure to go to the office each day. I was never bored or unhappy, and there was always some fun or frivolity to be had. Each year brought in new apprentices, and I was no longer the youngest person in the department. I would often tease the younger lads, but I never put anyone through the kind of hazing that I had endured. The other workers and I pulled lots of pranks on each other. Many of the older, married men used to play silly tricks on us younger guys. You'd never know what was around the corner. Those were fun times. One day, a few of us were sitting in the break room at lunchtime, setting up a prank for one of the older employees, when who should walk in but one of our senior managers. Of course, we all froze. He said, "What's going on here?" I replied, "Nothing! We're just having a bit of…recreation."

In this photo, I am in my early twenties, standing in the Taylors' backyard with the family cat.

He eyed me suspiciously for a moment and then said, "Well, carry on then." He turned on his heel and walked out. We really dodged one there! We played many tricks on one another, but they were always in good fun.

This snapshot captured a moment in time in my early twenties. Little did I know how swiftly my life was about to change.

As I approached my twenty-second birthday, the motorbike that I received from Albert and Nan played an important role in one of the most important encounters of my life. Albert and Nelson were also avid motorbike riders, and we all used to lock our bikes in a public rental garage near our house. One afternoon, as I was putting away my bike for the day, I noticed a young woman standing at a garage space a few doors down from mine. She was putting away a Lambretta, which is a little Italian motor scooter. She was absolutely striking. I was fascinated by this young woman who rode a motorbike and locked it in a public garage. I wanted to learn more about her, but I was too shy back then to introduce myself. Many days, I would wait at the garage, far from her unit, and watch for her. Then, I'm embarrassed to admit it, I would often follow after her, discreetly of course, to find out more about her. I never learned much. I figured that she must live nearby, but as I pursued her, she would always walk to the same row of shops, enter a radio repair store, and disappear.

Then one Saturday, the young woman and I happened to bump into one another outside of a bike shop. We had each gone there to get parts for our motorbikes, and that afternoon I lingered outside for a bit longer than usual to look at the parts that I had purchased. The shop door opened, and I looked up to see the same girl that I had been following for all these weeks. I knew that in a moment she would be on her way, and I might not get another chance to talk to her. I worked up the courage and started walking toward her. The words that came out of my mouth were, "Hi! How are you?" She stopped and turned round to look at me. "Fine," she said. I wasn't quite sure what to say next, so I walked up to her and asked, "What are you doing here?" She gave me a quizzical look and answered, "I am getting parts for my Lambretta. What are you doing here?" I answered her quickly, "I'm getting parts for my motorbike." There was a pause. By now, we were standing quite close. Then out of the blue, I blurted out, "Would you like to come round?" I was so nervous that I barely remember her response. I seem to recall she nodded and gave me a flash of a smile. There must have been an ensuing conversation, but I have no memory of what we said. All I know is that I came out of our chance encounter with the knowledge that her name was Beryl Kingston. Before I knew it, she was walking away from me, and I was left standing there with my thoughts racing.

When I recovered my composure, I thought to myself that this would be a perfect week for Beryl to come by, if indeed she chose to. My grandparents and Nelson were going to be away for several days, and I had the house to myself. I was relieved that I wouldn't get any awkward questions from my family if she did come to visit. Nelson was still teaching at my old primary school, and he had taken his pupils with him on holiday for a sailing trip. Albert and Nan were in America at the time visiting their daughter Joan, and they wouldn't be back until the following week.

The next evening, I was relaxing in the sitting room. I had a good friend over at the time, and we were sat on the sofa watching the TV. All of a sudden, I heard a knock at the front door. I got up to see who it was. When I opened the door, low and behold, there was the Lambretta girl, standing on my front step. I don't know who was more surprised that she had shown up, Beryl or me. I felt nervous to see her, but mostly elated, and I invited her to come in. I was glad that my friend was there. He helped break the tension and awkwardness between us. We watched TV and chatted long into the evening, and somewhat to my amazement, she wanted to come round again the next day.

She was sure taking a gamble, that's what I thought. I didn't think she knew what she was getting herself into. But unbeknownst to me, she had been talking to Grandfather Albert about me. She had noticed me at the bike garage, too, and she had struck up a conversation with Albert when I wasn't there. She was curious about who I was and where I had come from. Albert told her all about me. He described how the Taylors had rescued me from India, and he boasted about my apprenticeship with the London Electricity Board. After we had our first official date, I took her home to meet my family, and I was thoroughly confused when I saw that she already knew everybody. I asked, "What's going on here?" Grandfather laughed and said, "She already knows all about you, Joe. She's been asking us lots of questions." Beryl looked at me with a mischievous twinkle in her eye, and I couldn't help but burst out laughing. After all, it was delightful to learn that this young woman that I admired also fancied me! That was the start of our courtship and the beginning of a new chapter in my life.

Beryl was an enchanting companion, and the rest of my twenty-first year flew by in a revelry of fun and mischief. Before I knew it, my twenty-second birthday was at hand, and there were several important life milestones right around the corner. I graduated from technical college and received my diploma, and I also graduated from my apprenticeship. This meant that my Army deferment was now over, and I had to report for my conscription. The London Electricity Board offered me a full-time job as a draftsman, and they assured me that my position would be waiting for me when I returned from my two years of Army service.

At age twenty-two, diploma in hand, I showed up at the Army recruitment office. When I began the required training, I'd already had seven years of experience with the Sea Cadets, and I came to appreciate how well this education had prepared me for Army life. The Sea Cadets had drilled us like soldiers, and I already knew how to take care of myself and my equipment. Many of the other young men who were conscripted had no military background and didn't have the foggiest idea of what to do. For instance, when you received your kit, you had to mark every item in it with your name. This included your uniform, your boots, your gun, and everything else. If you didn't stencil your name on your equipment, another soldier would grab it, and you would look like a fool. However, if you had inscribed your name and you were missing something, all you had to do was tell the corporal, and he would find the person who had pinched it. There were stiff punishments for stealing each other's kit, so few people chanced nicking items that had been claimed.

A lot of the guys in my billet were young, scared, and inexperienced in a military setting. Most of them had recently turned eighteen, just one year out of boyhood. I realized that I could help them learn the ropes, so I became their unofficial mentor for a time. I taught them the culture and the unwritten rules of the Army. I showed the young men how to do firearm drills, how to march in parades, and how to tough out the dirty jobs that we were assigned. I showed them how to take orders shouted by the corporals and the sergeant major. These military personnel were strict and severe. They could bring you to tears. They would come right up to your face and challenge you. You would feel like yelling back, but you dared not because if you so much as looked at them wrong, you would be in serious trouble.

There's a saying that the Army will either make you or break you. I remember there was a young man who had recently immigrated from Africa. I felt sorry for him because he had just arrived in England, and he had a wife and child to support. He was going through severe culture shock. His English was quite good, and he was well-educated, but neither his wife nor his child could speak the language. He was worried sick because his wife didn't have any family nearby, so there was no one she could go to if she needed to ask for help. He would tremble and sweat with anxiety, and the rest of us tried to comfort him as best we could. He was such a nice man, and I got along with him quite well. The Army decided to discharge him before he had a nervous breakdown. They sent him back home to his wife and his kid. I was sorry to see him leave, but I was glad that he would be reunited with his family.

After fourteen days of basic training, it was time for my physical. If I passed this exam, I could begin more rigorous training that would prepare me for the infantry. I was ready to serve my two years. Unfortunately, I had a gammy leg, and I'd just had an operation on my left ankle and foot. The scar was starting to heal, but it was still red and raised. As I was standing in line for my physical, I heard the Army doctor say to someone, "Do not issue that man a uniform." I looked around and realized that the doctor was pointing his cane at me. I was crushed. I dearly wanted to go into the service. My adoptive country had given me a second chance at life, and I wanted an opportunity to give back. However, it wasn't to be. The doctor had good reason for discharging me. The other recruits would soon be doing intensive physical training on obstacle courses, and my leg would have made it difficult for me to keep up.

When I went back to my billet, I let the other recruits know what had happened. They were stunned that the Army had decided to discharge me. I had guided them through two challenging weeks, and they were all sad that I would be leaving. As I collected my things and got ready to depart, the lads in my billet decided they wanted to send me off with a farewell gift. We didn't earn much per day in the Army. Mind you, we didn't have to worry about buying much of anything because we had our lodging, food, and clothing all supplied to us. Still, any extra expenditure was a hardship. That made it all the more meaningful when these young men pooled what little resources they had and presented it to me in an envelope. I remember one of the guys said, "We really appreciate everything you've done for us. We want you to have this." Their gift brought a lump to my throat. I didn't want to take their money, but they insisted. They said it was their way of saying thanks. Their generosity gave me the means to pay for my travel home. Even though I wasn't able to join the Army myself, I was happy that I had been able to help those young men become soldiers.

After the Army discharged me, the Navy wrote to me and asked me if I would like to sign up for a nine-year tour. That seemed too long to me, and I turned it down. Later I thought, did I make a mistake? Should I have accepted it? But my job at the London Electricity Board was waiting for me. True to their word, the company was holding my job for me, even though they weren't expecting me to come back for another two years. When I showed up at work a few weeks later, they were all surprised. My coworkers asked me, "What are you doing here?" And I told them, "I got discharged from King and Country!" And that was that. My time in the military was over.

Now that I was back in London, I was glad that I had decided to return to civilian life. During my two weeks in the Army, Beryl and I had exchanged love letters back and forth, and it was clear that we were serious about each other. Beryl lived with her mum, her sister, and her brother in a flat above the radio repair shop where I used to watch her disappear in the days before our courtship began. Her mum and dad were separated. He had left when Beryl was around eight years old. He had served in the Air Force during the War, and when the War was over, he didn't return home except on odd occasions. He was a good man, he was just off on his own adventures, living his life according to his desires. Beryl and I courted for fourteen months before I finally got up the courage to ask her to marry me. When I popped the question, she didn't say "yes" or "no," which made me nervous at first. However, she explained that before she could agree to marry me, I had to go to her mum to ask her permission. Normally, you have to ask the father for his blessing to marry his daughter, but Beryl's dad was living in Cardiff, so I went to her mum instead. No sooner had I got the words out than she pulled me into a hug and enthusiastically welcomed me into the family. These were happy days. Beryl and I spent many afternoons riding our motorbikes together round the countryside. We were eager to tie the knot, and I was overjoyed at the prospect that an orphan boy like me could create a family of my very own with someone that I loved.

Before Beryl and I got married, however, there was something that I wanted to put right. My surname was still Miller, and I felt uncomfortable passing that name onto Beryl and our future children. In my mind, it was still associated with Mrs. Miller. I spoke to Nelson and told him that I wanted to make Taylor my last name. I wanted to fully become a Taylor, to honour the family that had rescued me and raised me as their own. Nelson looked at me for a moment, contemplating his reply. Then he said, "Joe, everybody knows you as Mr. Miller. I think you should stick with it. You can make it your own." At first, I was perturbed by Nelson's response; however, the more I thought about it, the more I realized that changing my name to Taylor was just a way of running from my past. Nelson was right. I could make my name my own. So, I decided that I would create a Miller family. I made the choice to repurpose and reclaim my name. I realized that this was more powerful than hiding from my history or trying to discard it. I would rewrite the story of the Miller name and give it new meaning. Mrs. Miller was now gone completely. As they say, water under the bridge. That name was now mine. Joe Miller. It is a fine name, really.

CHAPTER 12

The spring of 1958 rolled around, and Beryl and I were in the full swing of planning our wedding. We wanted to be married in late summer or early fall. We were looking forward to starting our life together, and I was already anticipating the arrival of children to our household. Finally, I would have a family of my own, one that belonged to me, one that I created.

Sadly, while Beryl and I grew closer, my adoptive family began to come apart. There were cracks forming in the Taylor household. Grandfather Albert had grown quite abusive toward Nan. He had always been harsh on her, but his behaviour had become crueler in recent years. Nelson was always the one who could keep Grandfather in check; however, he had recently moved out of the family home, and Grandfather's aggression had escalated. Nowadays, something would set him off, and he would turn and take it out on Nan.

Nan was my north star, my guiding light, and I couldn't bear to see her get hurt. Now that I was a man, nearly twenty-three years old, I was in a position to stand up for her. One evening, after yet another row, I confronted Grandfather. I strode up to him and said, "Don't you ever lay a hand on Nan again. If you do, you'll have to answer to me." Grandfather didn't like that I challenged him. At that time, I was quite fit, and he knew that I could have bested him physically if it came to that. I think that I scared him. He looked at me and said, "You don't belong in this family. Get out of this house."

I was stunned. I stood absolutely still, staring at him, but he didn't back down. He meant it. I turned and went to my room, unsure of what to do next. Nelson wasn't going to rescue me this time. I had to figure this out on my own.

I pulled out the trunk that I had brought with me on my long journey from India twelve years earlier. I opened the lid and began placing my belongings inside. I filled the trunk and several suitcases. Soon I had packed everything that was essential. I sat there awhile as my luggage stared blankly back at me. I was in a state of shock, but I knew I had to formulate a plan.

The next day, I reached out to several friends, all of whom agreed to take me in for a little while. I knew, however, that this was a short-term solution. I would have to find permanent lodgings, and fast. Grandfather had not relented. I would still have to leave home. Nan was quite upset because she didn't know where I was going to go. She worried that I might wind up homeless. She was such a good woman.

After all that she had endured, she was more concerned for my well-being than her own.

My old trunk is my one treasured possession from my life in India.

That was when Pip came to the rescue. Pip was a dear friend of Nan's. They had become quite close during the War when Nan invited Pip and her mum to use the family's air raid shelter. I knew that she lived alone in a little maisonette in London, so I thought she might not mind having a lodger. I reached out to her and asked if I could remain with her for a few weeks, but she told me that I could stay as long as I needed. She made me feel ever so welcome. "Don't worry," I reassured Nan. "Pip will take me in."

To this day, it hurts me that Grandfather turned me out. After being adopted as a child and living with the Taylors for twelve years, I was wounded to my core when he told me that I didn't belong in the family. All I had done was stand up to him in order to protect the woman who was for all intents and purposes my mother. It took me many years to forgive Grandfather for that.

I stayed at Pip's flat for months, all throughout my wedding planning with Beryl. Pip was a high-end clothing designer. She worked with some of the top brands, dreaming up fashionable dresses for London's high society. When she found out that Beryl and I were to be wed that year, she told us that she wanted to design Beryl's bridal gown for the occasion. She offered this as her present to us, and to our amazement, she refused to take even a penny for the dress. She knew that we were both struggling to get by. She told us that she would even create a bridesmaid's dress for Beryl's sister, Penny. Without Pip's love and kindness, I know that Beryl and I would have experienced much greater hardship in that period of our lives together.

Our wedding took quite a bit of planning. One major obstacle we had to overcome was how to unite our differing religions. I had been baptized Roman Catholic at Saint Joseph's Orphanage, and Mrs. Miller had adopted and kept me because she wanted a Catholic house boy. Perhaps as a half-Indian lady, she wanted to distinguish herself and her household from the predominantly Hindu inhabitants of Jamshedpur. In Father Comerford's correspondence with Nelson, the priest had made it clear that my adoption away from Mrs. Miller was contingent on the Taylors maintaining my faith, even though they belonged to the Church of England. True to his word, Nelson had raised me Roman Catholic and had never sought to baptize me into the Anglican faith.

Beryl was raised Presbyterian, and the church where we were to be married was the Kingston family's congregation in London. Tensions between Catholics and Protestants were at an all-time low after the War. The threat of Nazi occupied Britain had brought these former enemies together as they fought for a common cause. Regardless, we realized we still needed to talk to Beryl's minister and get his permission for us to be wed.

I had attended a few services at the Kingstons' congregation, and I remembered that the minister seemed to like me. I tried to remind myself of this to abate my nerves as we met with the man who had the power to grant us the church's blessing. The minister greeted us with a smile and a handshake. Then he turned to me and said, "Son, no matter what religion you are, you are most welcome in this church." I felt the relief wash over me. This was no small gesture. This man could have branded me an outsider. A Catholic, an Indian, a foreigner. He could have required me to convert or told us to find a different church for our wedding. Instead, he chose to embrace me and welcome me into the fold. Beryl and I were overjoyed. We set the date of our ceremony for 20th September, three days before the start of the autumn season. Our minister read the banns in the congregation, and I remember how happy I felt as the community congratulated us on taking this next big step in our lives together.

Here I am with some of my mates. We are dressed for a game of cricket, my favourite sport. I am the chap in the front row seated furthest to the left.

The months sped by, and spring turned to summer. August waxed and waned and brought with it my twenty-third birthday. Before I could bat an eye, September was upon us. Nervous excitement makes time move at a breakneck pace. A couple weeks before the big day, some of my coworkers at the London Electricity Board arranged for me to have a bachelor's night out. By now, I had formed a core group of friends at my workplace. We were all in our mid-twenties, and we would often get together outside of work and have a cracking good time. For my bachelor's party, they said, "Come on, Joe, let's go have a bash. Let's go to the West End. That's where the life is." Just like today, the West End of the 1950s was home to London's theatres and cinemas. My mates and I headed to Piccadilly Circus for a night out. We had dinner and drinks, and while some of the lads let loose, I was more careful. I made sure not to imbibe enough to get well and truly drunk. After dinner, we went to see a movie. While I don't remember the film, I do recall the stroll we took afterwards. The group of us started walking and reminiscing, and eventually some of the lads made sure we wound up in the seedy part of town. They were keen to visit the red-light district.

While I was still planning my bachelor's party, I distinctly remember that the father of one of my mates had come to me and said, "Joe, when you are out on the town, you best make sure my son does not get involved with one of those ladies." I thought, "How am I going to do that? I'm not his babysitter. What if he disappears on us?" I promised, however, that I would look out for him.

In London, it's almost always cold and raining, and that night was no exception. As we walked along, we could see burlesque dancers standing outside of the nightclubs that lined the street, huddling under umbrellas and having a smoke. As if on cue, my friend gestured as if he wanted to visit one of the clubs. I shook my head. "No, no, you can run over and have a quick chat, but that's as far as you're going." He eagerly trotted over to one of the women and tried to strike up a conversation. She didn't ignore him, but it was clear that she wanted to finish her cigarette and go back inside. I waved to him and called his name. "Alright, let's go. Come on then." I made sure that he tagged along with us after that. If he disappeared, there would be no way of getting him back home with his dignity intact. I shook my head and chuckled, breathing a sigh of relief. I would still be able to look his father in the eye after that night.

The week leading up to our wedding was beautiful September weather. The rain and damp that had started the month gave way to balmy temperatures and sunny skies, at least sunny for London. Lucky for us, Beryl's father was home from the forces, and we were able to use his car to run errands in preparation for the ceremony. I had never met him before that, and I hadn't known what to expect. Spousal separation wasn't that common at the time, and even though Beryl's mum and dad weren't divorced, it was clear that he was not planning on returning home to London to live with the family. I had been expecting to meet someone brusque or aloof, but instead he was a jovial man with a warm smile. He shook my hand and welcomed me into the family. His acceptance of me was an unexpected blessing. From being a lonely orphan boy, I was now gaining a new father.

Pip had come through as promised. She created the most exquisite dress for Beryl to wear. It was an ankle-length white gown that was beautifully decorated with gold leaf. I remember I couldn't keep my eyes off of Beryl. I was well and truly smitten. Our wedding photograph perfectly captures my state of mind that day. In the image, Beryl is smiling squarely at the camera while I gaze blissfully at her, lost in the moment and utterly in love.

We had a large reception. In addition to our families, we had invited our friends and work colleagues. Some of them were from my job, some were from Beryl's workplace, and others were friends that we had made through our motorbike club.

My wedding to Beryl was one of the happiest days of my life. To think that an orphan like me could live to experience such joy!

I was glad to see many of my chums from the London Electricity Board in attendance. My best man, Ron Legend, was one of my best mates at work. I realized I would now be joining the ranks of family men. What a life change! I could hardly believe it. Less than fifteen years before, I had been an orphan surviving on the streets of India. Now I was a newly married man, standing beside my wife, cheered on by friends and family, surrounded by love. It was a beautiful day.

Unfortunately, the Taylors and the Kingstons sat apart that day. They didn't mix like families normally do at a wedding. As happy as the occasion was, we noticed certain tensions building throughout the day. As the sun rose in the sky and morning turned to afternoon, Beryl and I were glad to get away. We cut the cake, and then we took off on our honeymoon.

We had decided on Bournemouth as our honeymoon destination. Bournemouth is a beautiful resort town in the South of England that overlooks the English Channel. Beryl's mum had helped us find lodgings there. She had a good friend who lived in the town and had a guest room that could accommodate two. That evening, we turned up on her doorstep after a three-hour train ride from London, luggage in hand and weary looks on our faces. She welcomed us in with a warm smile and a twinkle in her eye. We were both knackered, and all we wanted to do was get some rest so we could explore the town the next day.

As we awoke in the morning, I felt a thrill as I realized that this was our first full day with each other as husband and wife. We were in love and delighted to have this time to spend together. We decided to go exploring. Bournemouth was beautiful and we wanted to drink our fill before we had to return to the dreariness of London. The weather that day was balmy if somewhat overcast, and the breeze that wafted through the town smelled of sea spray. We strolled through little shops with pretty knickknacks, and then we made our way to Bournemouth Gardens where couples sat picnicking amongst the last flowers of the season. As we continued our jaunt, our feet carried us down to the pier. We walked onto the beach, which was dotted with families enjoying the final days of summer. Children splashed in the waves and made sandcastles along the beach. I smiled at Beryl and felt my heart beat faster as I realized that our children would soon be playing on a beach just like this, building sandcastles and watching the tide carry them away.

We walked hand-in-hand along the shore, people-watching and chatting. We smiled at the children who ran along the beach, searching for seashells and driftwood to place inside of little tin pails. Off in the surf, we could see children and teens bobbing and sputtering as they dunked each other in the waves.

After an hour or so, grey clouds started to roll in and the wind picked up. The waves became choppy, and some parents pulled their protesting children back onto dry land. We could feel the sea spray on our faces mixed with the smell of oncoming rain. It was now getting close to dinnertime, and we decided to escape the weather and walk into town for a meal. We chose a little pub down the street from a cinema. We figured that we might pop in to see a movie later. We had a lovely dinner, but toward the end of our meal, we could hear the pitter-patter of raindrops outside. As I paid the bill, we braced ourselves for what would be a sprint to our next destination. We scurried outside, and the heavens seemed to open and unleash the flood they had been threatening all day. Beryl and I looked at each other and started giggling. So much for escaping the London drizzle on our honeymoon!

We raced down the street to the little cinema, trying as best we could to dry ourselves under the awning before we queued up for our tickets. Many of the filmgoers in the queue were as bedraggled as we were. Clearly, we were not the only couple who had sought refuge at the cinema. A rainy night made for good business. We had been in such a rush to get out of the downpour that we hadn't even managed to glance at the marquee. We were ready to see whatever might be playing so long as it gave the rain time to slow to a manageable drizzle. That was when we heard the couple ahead of us ask for tickets to *The Ten Commandments*. Beryl and I looked at each other. What a treat! We had of course heard of the film, but we hadn't yet been able to see it. It had premiered in 1956, but it had only recently received a wide release. We stepped up to the window and got two tickets. I think I paid 25p in total. What a bargain! We walked into the cinema, still shaking water from our clothes, and made our way to the usher who showed us to our seats.

What a night that was! I still remember the sweeping scale of the film. Beryl and I watched in awe as Charlton Heston's Moses raised his staff and the waters of the Red Sea reared up to allow the Israelites to flee. As I watched the story unfold, I felt some identification with Moses. Here was an orphan boy whose birth mother was forced to send him into the unknown, hoping that he might survive to have a better life. He grew up not knowing his true parentage, adopted by a family who loved him as their own, and yet hubris ultimately drove them apart. For as long as I could remember, I had hungered for a family to call my own. The Taylors had answered my prayers and saved me from destitution, but now Nelson was busy with his work and Albert had given me his ultimatum. Albert and I were cordial with each other now, but the relationship we'd had before was forever changed. I looked over at Beryl. She was my kindred now. Together, we would create a family that I could truly call my own.

We returned from our honeymoon and began our married life together. Within a few months, Beryl gave me the news that I had been hoping for ever since we got married. She was pregnant! I could barely contain my joy. We told Pip straightaway, and she was thrilled for us. She did whatever she could to make us comfortable and cozy. Beryl and I were both working at the time. I had my draftsman job at the London Electricity Board, and Beryl was a comptometer operator at a construction company. A comptometer was a mechanical adding machine, like a simple calculator. It allowed her to keep track of the workmen's wages and do other secretarial tasks. Once she learned that she was pregnant, she decided it was best for her to leave her job. This was commonplace for women in the workplace at the time. I realized this would mean a cut in our family wages, and it was a struggle at first to live on a single income. Beryl intended to go back to work once our child was old enough, but we had to tighten our belts and spend our money even more frugally.

Once you get married, your life changes completely. Sometimes I would think to myself, "Where did all my freedom go? I'm married, and soon I'll have a wife and child to support." Then I would remember, I'd had my share of fun during my bachelor years. Now was the time for me to grow into the responsible husband and father that my burgeoning family needed me to be.

We had the upstairs suite in Pip's maisonette, and as Beryl's pregnancy progressed, she was finding that going up and down the stairs was becoming increasingly difficult. Thank goodness for our friends and workmates. We would invite them over to run errands. They would come by and bring us gifts and help with everyday tasks. The spring of 1959 blossomed into summer. We began preparing our flat for our baby, who was due to be born at the end of October. Beryl sold her Lambretta in order to afford a pram. I still had my motorbike, but it was a one-seater, so she couldn't ride on the back. We would invite our friends from the motorbike club over for tea or dinner, and they would return the favour by doing our shopping or giving Beryl a lift when she had an appointment.

As the summer of 1959 waned, Beryl and I celebrated my twenty-fourth year, followed by the one-year anniversary of our marriage. After our anniversary, Beryl's belly seemed to grow by the day, and we knew that we had no more than a month to prepare for our first child. We purchased a crib and decorated the baby's room. Even the guys in the office decided to participate, in their own fashion of course. They held a raffle to guess how much the baby would weigh. Judging by

Beryl's increasing size and discomfort, I reckoned the winner would be whoever bet the highest number.

The 23rd October began as a regular Friday morning. I awoke, got ready for work, and gave a groggy and uncomfortable Beryl a kiss goodbye. I arrived at the London Electricity Board, clocked in, and sat down at my drafting table. As I began drawing the plan of the electricity grid that my team was working on, I was notified that I had an urgent phone call. My heart jumped into my throat, and I rushed to see who was on the other line. Hands shaking, I picked up the receiver. It was the hospital. Beryl had gone into labour that morning. I hastily informed my manager that Beryl was giving birth, and I ran outside. I grabbed my motorbike and raced to the hospital. The trip should have taken me forty-five minutes, and I made it in thirty. I have never driven so fast on a motorbike before or since.

I arrived at the hospital at Clapham Common, sweaty and out of breath. I wanted to see Beryl, but it was not customary for husbands to be in the delivery room. Beryl also told me later that she had instructed the nurses, "Do not let Joe in the room. He won't be able to take the sight of blood." She was right, of course. I probably would have fainted.

While Beryl was delivering our baby, I stood in the hallway, pacing back and forth. Across the hall there was a nursery for newborns to receive care while their mothers recuperated from labour. A large glass window allowed families to gaze at these new additions to their clan. I stared at the rows upon rows of infants in their little bassinets, and I couldn't help thinking to myself, "Why, these are all so ugly!" I started to worry that my baby would be strange looking too. I needn't have worried, though. God in His wisdom has ensured that parents will always find their child to be the most beautiful sight in the world.

Later that day, Beryl gave birth to our firstborn, a bouncing baby boy. The nurse invited me back to see him, and I had to restrain myself from rushing into the delivery room. I was overcome with wonder and delight. He was lying on Beryl's chest making little squawking noises. I looked at him and thought to myself, "Why, he is perfect!" He was a big baby. Nine pounds, fourteen ounces, to be exact. Somewhere in the back of my mind, I made a note to congratulate my mate, Ron Legend, who had entered our workplace raffle with the seemingly preposterous prediction of ten pounds.

Beryl and I had chosen the name Mark Joseph Miller. Mark was a Biblical name that we both liked, and Joseph showed respect to the convent that had fostered me. This name also celebrated the miracle of my survival, for it was a miracle that I had lived to have a son, this little child who would ensure that my story would not end with me.

I held little Mark in my arms. He blinked his eyes and made funny, puckered faces with his tiny mouth. The thought came to me that this was the first time I had ever really owned anything. I came from nothing, and now I had created something that was fully mine. This little child belonged to me. He was my first true family, my own blood.

I would never know my mother or my father. I would never have siblings or cousins who looked like me. But now, thanks to Beryl, this amazing woman who had chosen to be my soulmate, I had a son. This was a landmark moment in my life, my twenty-four-year odyssey. I didn't have a family, so I built my own. My family is my most treasured creation.

Here I am with my son, Mark Joseph Miller. Beryl is to the right of the photo, and her stepmum is sat between us. For the first time in my life, I finally had a family of my own.

I dedicate my story to my son Mark and my daughter Tanya. You have given me the greatest gift in the world, the gift of being a father. You are my pride and joy. All my love to you.

EPILOGUE: MARK MILLER

My name is Mark Miller, and I am my dad Joe's firstborn child. Like many kids do, when I was growing up, I thought my parents were both completely normal. That changed when I was about ten years old. The first inkling I got that there was anything different about my dad came when I realized that my mum had grandparents, but my dad didn't. Nelson was part of our lives, of course, but I knew that he was not my dad's father. I thought this was unusual, so I asked my dad about his childhood. He told me about being an orphan in India and running away from home. He kept most of the harrowing details from me until I was older, but it was enough for me to grasp just how unique my dad's upbringing had been.

When I was in my twenties, I found out that my mum had started to write a story about my dad's life. When I read what she had written, I was amazed by what my dad had been through. His life was even more incredible than what I had imagined as a child. I knew that we would have to get my dad to write his memoir one day. But then I got busy with my life, and my dad was working about ten different jobs as usual, and we never could seem to find the time to get his story down on paper.

It wasn't until I became a father myself that I understood how important my dad's story really is. My three sons, Joey, Jordon, and Justin would ask their Bapa questions about his life, and he would tell them about running away from Mrs. Miller, riding the trains across India, and meeting Nelson for the first time. My dad's life was the most amazing adventure I had ever heard. I saw how much his story resonated with my sons, how it gave them so much hope and strength, and I knew that we had to share his story with the world.

I finally convinced my dad to write his memoir. What you now hold in your hands is Part I of what will ultimately be two books. My dad's adventures didn't stop after he had me, quite the contrary. He continued to persevere despite many challenges and obstacles in his path. A few years after I was born, my parents brought my sister Tanya into the world. We were now a family of four, and my dad knew that he would not be able to support our growing family on a draftsman's salary. As he had done since he was a little child, he picked himself up and moved forward. He moved the family to Wales and eventually to Canada, following wherever work led him.

In Canada, my sister Tanya and I both built families of our own. I have my three sons, and Tanya has a daughter, Aysia. Despite tremendous odds, my dad has ensured that his lineage and his story will not end with him. He has built three generations under the Miller name, a name that he reclaimed for himself. We may not be able to trace his ancestry back in time and uncover the full story of his origins, but in the end, asking the question "Who Am I?" is not about digging into the past. It is about building a self, an identity. My dad has achieved that. He is a husband, a father, a grandfather, and one day, he will be a great-grandfather. He has created a strong family that will continue his legacy forward into the future.

APPENDIX: LETTERS AND DOCUMENTS

The following original letters and documents from India and London are transcribed in the chapters above. After each scanned page in this appendix, I have provided the page number in the book where you can read the letter in context.

Return to Padre

St Mary's Church
Jamshedpur
21-1-45

Dear F. Buckley,

I am so glad to get news of that boy Joseph Miller. His history is the following: He was adopted by a certain Mr Mrs Miller (Catholics) of Golmuri Jamshedpur & up to about a year or two ago proved incorrigible. Mrs Miller shed tears in my presence at what she called the boy's ingratitude. He couldn't be corrected for he would abscond for a day or more. If sent on a message to buy household needs he would spend a much longer time than needed with the Indian bazaar brats & then had a habit of nipping a few coins (pice) from the sum he received for the purchases. (I think she also referred to a gambling propensity). At any rate he was punished, absconded & [illegible] let him stay away. I made enquiries & found a trace. I thought that he was still somewhere in my neighbourhood.

This boy Joseph is an adopted son of Mrs Miller given to them by the Chandernagore Convent when a baby. Mrs Miller will be pleased to hear that he is being cared for & follows the Catholic faith. She will make no claim on him. According whoever has won the youngster's good will & is pre[illegible] to train him & to educate him

Letter from Father J. Comerford to Reverend B. T. Buckley. 21st January 1945. Page 1. See pages 41-43.

as a Catholic may assume the full title of guardian.
Besides if my register records him which I doubt, there
is a Joseph Miller born 4th May 1926 but no reference to
adoption. This date makes him much too old. His baptismal
record is probably to be found in St Joseph's Convent
Chandernagore as the nuns have a creche for little
orphan children & doubtless baptise them as soon as
they receive their tiny charges.

If then the R A F man has taken to him & the boy
responds, you will probably agree with me to let the
youngster continue in his charge is a splendid
solution. If you be good enough to let me know
something of the youngster even in his future career
I shall be very pleased. Mrs Miller too will be
delighted to know that what she found impossible
some one else has succeeded in. She was fond of the
boy but had to relinquish all claim to him when
he proved so insubordinate in her care.

Are you the same Buckley who was attached
to the Cuttack parish or are you straight from
Europe? With all good wishes fully reciprocated
& I shall not forget to offer for you a prayer
or memento at holy mass for success in your difficult
work.

Yours sincerely in Xt
J Comerford SJ

Letter from Father J. Comerford to Reverend B. T. Buckley. 21st January 1945. Page 2. See pages 41-43.

St. Joseph's Convent,
Chandernagore.
9th April '45.

Father Buckley

Dear Reverend Father,

In answer to your letter I shall try and tell you as much as I can gather from our Register about the Boy in question.

His Mother was a Bengalee and his Father is said to be a pure European. The Mother died and left her son to a Bengalee friend who brought him to our Orphanage when he was 3 years old. He was taken over on the 15th August 1935 and was baptised "Joseph" on the 20th August '35. Mrs. Miller, an Anglo-Indian lady from Tatanager called at our Indian Orphanage in view of adopting a child and took a great fancy to Joe. He left with her on the 12th June 1938 and we heard nothing more about him.

Joseph seemed quite out of place with the other little Indian children in our Orphanage and we were so pleased when Mrs. Miller gave him a Home.

I am very pleased to know that Joseph is now in a good College and hope and pray he will give every satisfaction.

May I recommend our Community & Boarding School to your good prayers.

Yours respectfully in J. C.

Mother Marie Agnes Superior

St. Joseph's Convent,
Chandernagore,
4- 8- '45.

Corporal or Sargent

Dear ~~Captain~~ Taylor,

I am pleased to do my best to tell you all I know of the little boy in question. He came to us on the 15th August 1935, and seemed to be at least 3 years of age, he was able to run about everywhere and had to be watched continually. He may of course have been only two years old. He was baptised on the 20th August and was called Joseph. He remained with us for about a year and then Mrs Miller took a great fancy to him and asked to adopt him.

Joseph's Mother was a pure Indian and the Father a European, either English or Scotch. When we take over a child into our Orphanage he cannot be reclaimed and therefore we make very few inquiries about the parentage.

I thank you for your very nice letter and I hope Joseph will always be grateful and repay you for all your kindness.

Yours sincerely

Mother Marie Agnes
Superior

Letters from Mother Marie Agnes, Mother Superior of St. Joseph's Convent in Chandannagar, India to Father Buckley and Nelson Taylor. 8th and 9th April 1945. See page 3 and pages 44-45.

St Mary's Church
Jamshedpur
6. 4. 45

Dear Cpl. Taylor

I am more than gratified at hearing your account & your intentions regarding Joe Miller. I am convinced that he will prove grateful to you for all you are doing for him. You ought to remind him not to let die a spark of gratitude for his first adopting parents – Mr & Mrs Miller. They brought him up from babyhood & treated him as their own child. They supplied all his needs & such personal effort should not be without a response in the recipient. Mrs Miller shed tears in my presence when she had to relinquish all hope of controlling the boy. She will be very pleased to hear that he is safe.

I made enquiries about him round here & I was about to examine a locality where he was last seen when the letter reached me that he had been taken on by you. Now I shall convey your message to Mr & Mrs Miller who will be indeed pleased to know that Joe will be educated & brought up in his Catholic faith.

With all good wishes
Yours sincerely
J Comerford

Letter from Father J. Comerford to Nelson Taylor. 6th April 1945. See pages 46-47.

SOCIETY FOR THE PROTECTION OF CHILDREN
IN INDIA

Phone No. Pk. 2077. 2B, Camac Street,

Calcutta, 7th May, 1945.

1429693 Cpl.Taylor, N.D.,
7082. Servicing Echelon.,
C/o R. A. R.,
Imphal.

Dear Mr. Taylor,

Joseph Miller: 6790.

Thank you for your letter of the 26th ultimo regarding the above-named boy. We have placed on record the particulars supplied by you which are much the same as obtained by us from the Convent direct.

We have been assured by the Convent that there is no claimant for the boy, and we therefore see no objection to your adopting him and arranging for his welfare as outlined in your original letter to us.

We shall nevertheless welcome periodical reports regarding the boy's progress and welfare if you can possibly arrange this.

With all good wishes,

Yours sincerely,

Neal Davidson

GENERAL SECRETARY.

AMC/GCD.

Letter from The Society for the Protection of Children in India to Nelson Taylor. 7th May 1945. See pages 47-48.

Sunday, 20th May, '45. 120, Topsham Road,

My Dear Son,

I wrâte to you on Tuesday last but we had another letter from you yesterday, it was here when I arrived home from work(?), dated 9th May, with the two snaps enclosed. Old Lad you look tired & sad and it is not very cheering to see you looking like that. I should think that it is nearly time that you were hearing about coming home yourself, just how do you stand on the list now Son?, Have you any idea?

I have had no news yet from the Welfare but have every hopes. Do your best to let me have that information about you & Joey as soon please Son and then I shall be able to 'gate crash' into their hives again without waiting for them to send for me.

I guess that you feel a bit 'fed' now that the news from here of war is finished but I do not think that your area will supply war news for a à lot longer. Never fear Old Son we keep our mind very much on your Area News, it is true that we do not get so much of it splashed across the paper headlines but there are some thousands of people at home with relatives out your way who are eager for what little is doled out for us to read.

John is up for the week end and at present your nephew J.R. is being filled up with Robb's Biscuit, it is about 16.45., and by the sound of things, there is a bit of an argument going on as to whether he should finish it all or not. I expect that Joan will win. We, John & I, took him out this morning for a run and just beat the rain in getting home again. It has been pouring all the afternoon but appears to be lifting a bit now. The garden looks a lot better for it and I have no doubt that the flowers & veg. will be that so much better for we have had quite a dry spell.

Mum was down looking at her strawberries just before lunch and is already talking about how much jam she will be able to make against you two coming home, Lord Woolton approving. I say that because there is a lot of talk of a cut in the sugar ration, heaven knows that we do not get overburdened with sweetstuffs as it is but I suppose that we must think of the poor germans who will have to go without if we do not accept a cut. That, perhaps, is an unfair thing to say but it seems odd to me that we have managed pretty well so far but as soon as the war in Europe à is finished so a shortage occurs in many of the essentials. Roll on that Election perhaps then we shall be able to put things right but I've almost given up hope for this country, cant and vested interest appear to be pretty rife. I can only hope that you Lads will be strong enough to make yourselves heard when you return.

Letter from Albert Taylor to Nelson Taylor. 20th May 1945. Page 1. See pages 50-52.

COPY

Air Ministry, D.A.F.W.
160, Ashley Gardens,
S.W. 1.

166/A.F.W.2(a)

18th May, 1945.

Dear Sir,

1429693 Cpl. N. D. Taylor.

With reference to your call on the 12th instant and our conversation regarding the adopted boy of your son, I think I should advise you that, as I understand the English law, legal adoption cannot be effected unless there is a difference of not less than 21 years between the ages of your son and the boy. I believe that English law applies to India but it would be as well for your son to look into this aspect of his problem, as, if legal adoption cannot be arranged it may alter the whole situation.

When your son returns to U.K. I do not think there will be any difficulty about bringing the boy with him and if he applies to the Command through his Commanding Officer they would probably embark the boy on the same vessel..

The boy would require docùments in order to enter U.K. and your Son should get in touch with the Home Department of the Provincial Goverment á in which he is stationed who would issue the necessary passport or identity documents, etc. Although the boy is a British subject he must be in possession of these papers before embarking so they must be obtained in India.

As regards the fare, if the boy is permitted to travel home in the same troopship as your son and is provided with third class accommodation the cost of the passage at half rate would be £17.10.

Civilians, however, are not normally permitted to travel third class on troopships and if the boy returns unaccompanied the cost of his fare at 2nd class rates would be £23. 10.

As the airman is unmarried he is precluded form the grant of a passage at public expense.

Perhaps I should point out again that the important problem at the moment is the legal of the boy as the above remarks would not apply if the courts fefuse the application in which case I do not think there would be any prospect of bringing the boy to England. If I can be of any further assistance, please do not hesitaee to get in touch with me. (over)

Letter from D. V. Tandy, RAF Air Ministry, to Albert Taylor. 18th May 1945.

See pages 52-53.

Monday, 21st May '45.

As you can see, I did notfinish this yesterday so here I am again. I did not expect that there would be a post delivery this morning but there was one and I had a letter from Welfare and I'll make out a copy and enclose it with this. One piece of the info. is a little disturbing, but you must take up enquiries right away and let me know the result. The point in question is the difference in age and if that is a difficulty I think that you had better name me as the person and I'll give you full power to act for me but be careful as the snag about getting him to this country might present more difficulties. Anyhow I'll leave it to you to act as you think best but you have my permission to use my name as far as you think fit in order to get this laddie settled with a view to him coming to this country.

I think that this is about all for this week Son, So will close down for now. Let me have some info. as soon as you possibly can. Cheerio Old Son, God Bless You and take care of you. All at Home send Love and Best Wishes. Cheerio! Happy Landings!

Dad.

Letter from Albert Taylor to Nelson Taylor. 21st May 1945. Page 2. See page 54.

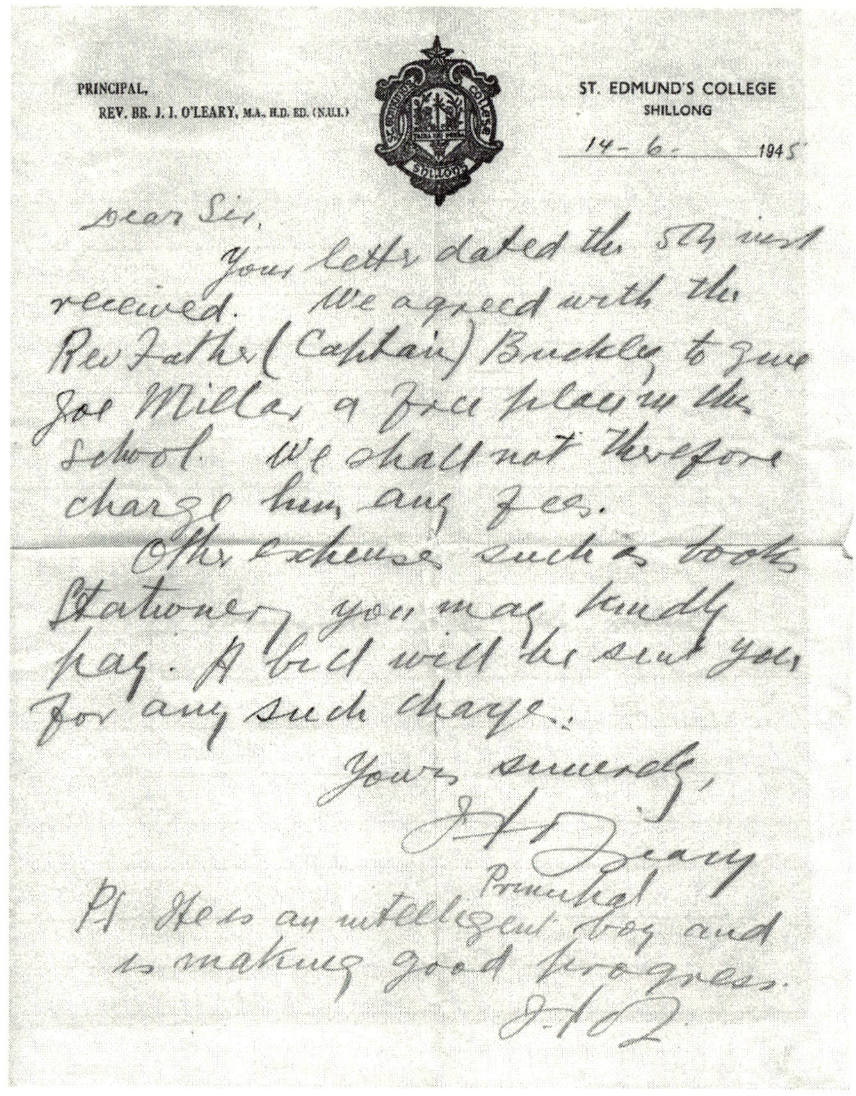
PRINCIPAL,
REV. BR. J. I. O'LEARY, M.A., H.D. ED. (N.U.I.)

ST. EDMUND'S COLLEGE
SHILLONG

14-6-1945

Dear Sir,

Your letter dated the 5th inst received. We agreed with the Rev Father (Captain) Buckley to give Joe Miller a free place in the school. We shall not therefore charge him any fees.

Other expenses such as books stationery you may kindly pay. A bill will be sent you for any such charges.

Yours sincerely,

J. I. O'Leary
Principal

P.S. He is an intelligent boy and is making good progress.
J. I. O'L

Letter from Father J. I. O'Leary, Principal of St. Edmund's College in Shillong, to Nelson Taylor. 14th June 1945. See pages 59-60.

Rev. B.T.Buckley, 161026,
232 Group, R.A.F.,
June 15th. '45.

Dear Cpl. Taylor,

Your letter has just arrived, it has taken ten days: nearly twice as long as a letter from Blighty.

From the above (not the sketch!) you see I have been posted. I was on my way to the old Wing when, in passing through Calcutta, I heard of my posting here.

I am very upset by your letter, by the refusal of Fr. Ricaldone to hand over the money and half of the kit with Joe. I am just waiting to heqr whether another Catholic RAF chaplain has been sent to Shillong, as was expected of Fr. White whose health is poor; but if he has not gone there, I shall consider Shillong still within the bounds of my jurisdiction; and therefore I shall visit the place as soon as possible. While up there I shall thrash out matters in no vague terms with both the Bishop and Fr. Ricaldone and see that Joe gets satisfaction. Should Fr. White be posted there, I shall send a letter to the Bishop with a copy to Fr. Ricaldone and ask for immediate action; failing which, I shall write to the Superior Provincial of the Salesians - a friend of mine - and get him to step in. He must have understood the initial amount to be a voluntary donation; that is feasible; but that the boy's kit should be considered common property is just a little far-fetched. However, I shall demand ₨ 150/- plus the complete outfit. It is surprising that Fr. Ricaldone has not written to me.

Are you at the same place as Cpl Conway (sports wallah) now? I dropped down from the blue some days ago, but had only a couple of hours in which to run ffom pillar to post trying to get my things and did not succeed fully. If you see Cpl. Conway, tell him I have received his letter, written to Fr. Ulyatt; that I ~~have~~ took with me the harmonium wrapped up in the rug, the box of missals and a wooden box of books from stores, but am waiting for

Letter from Reverend B. T. Buckley to Nelson Taylor. 15th June 1945. Page 1. See pages 60-61.

the two tin trunks. My church account book and other things required for "clearing up" at 908 Wing are in the trunks, so until I receive these I cannot satisfy the "complaints".

Hoping matters will straighten out concerning Joe and that you will have the pleasure of taking him home with you soon,

I remain,

Yours sincerely in Our Lord

B. T. Buckley

Letter from Reverend B. T. Buckley to Nelson Taylor. 15th June 1945. Page 2. See page 61.

Sunday, 24th June,'45. 120, Topsham Road,
London, S.W. 17.

My Dear Son,

We have had two letters from you this week and the packet containing Joey's letters. The letters were dated 15/6 & 18/6 respectively. Someone is obviously pulling a finger out in the matter of mail coming in this direction, I wish that the same could be said about mail coming out to you. However I suppose that it will all right itself oneday but roll on that day when we shall not have to write to you.

You gave me quite a shock in the first of these letters, with the postcript from Jane. I began to think that you had started a nursery or some such but the second letter cleared the air a little and I assume that Jane is a friend of Joey's. Then I thought that 'Our Jane' of the Daily Mirror had deserted us for the SEAC but that is not the case.

Well Old Lad we were pleased to hear that the parcel had arrived safely, I was a little worried about it as we read so much of packets for the Far East 'going astray' and no arriving at their destination. So you are pleased with the parcel, I'm glad that it has pleased you, I'll get all that I can for you but unless you ask I shall not dispatch any more for a while. We have a lovely little Flannel Suit here for him, I think that I mentioned this in a previous letter, and Mum is well away with the pulover but if you want it sent you must say. You see Son, in spite of you volunteering for that extra year, we both think that you will be home before that time and we do not want to send parcels out with you on the way home. Understand?.

Now Old Lad about this money question, I want to try to explain my outlook and maybe it will be a little difficult to put into this letter but I want you to understand that at all times, as far as I am concerned your happiness and peace of mind are my first consideration, that is as far as you are concerned. This money must not be allowed to worry you at all and it is there for you to use as YOU think fit. Joan is away for this week-end but as soon as she can manage, I'll get her to put a futther £10 to the credit of Mr. Mellish but I have a further suggestion to make to you and I'd like an answer as soon as you can let me have it. Would you like me to put a larger sum, say £50 to your credit out at one of the Banks in India. It is only a suggestion and to my mind it would appear to have several advantages. By this means you would always have a sense of security where cash is concerned and a means of not worrying yourself about getting from home. After all Son, you are free, white & 21 and therefore quite capable of thinkingfor yourself and it is YOUR MONEY that you are dealing with. I don't want you to think that I do not want the trouble of dealing with these affairs for you but Old Lad as afr as is possible I want to stop you worrying. This last letter is very much like a youngster asking for a penny to spend and I want you to get above that, I'm not condemning you for that so please don't let that enter your mind. Money is only useful for the happiness it will bring, think that out sometime, that is my outlook on money and if it will serve that purpose then use it and don't worry. I hope that I have made that clear without giving you cause to grieve but if you do feel a little annoyed, well Lad go back to the beginning of this paragraph and read that again. O.K?.

Letter from Albert Taylor to Nelson Taylor. 24th June 1945. Page 1. See pages 62-65.

I expect that you will wonder how Joan enters into the question of remitting money out to you. Well she hasa banking A/c. with the National & Provincial at Tooting Broadway and that is the easiest way of dealing with this problem. I get Mum to draw out from the P.O. A/c. and pay Joan back that way. I am friendly with the Manager of this branch, he is Treasurer to the Unit Committee and is always ready to help all he can in these matters. The first remmitances I sent were sent during the time I had the Unit's A/c. under my signature but that is no longer the case and I'm very glad about it as I'll explain to you when I see you and when we get a chance for a 'gabfest'.

Joan had a cable from Austin on Friday, he is back in the States and, according to his wire, is going to go all out to get Joan plus J.R. out there as soon as he can. Knowing him and the way in which he can put over a 'hard luck' story, I expect that it will not be long before she gest her 'sailing orders'.

Letter from Albert Taylor to Nelson Taylor. 24th June 1945. Page 2. See pages 62-65.

I have not had the chance to get along to a Public Notary as yet but I will do so as soon as I possibly can. This is for the power of Attorney of course. The difficulty is getting away from work as there are no offices open when I'm finished work(?) in the evening.

We have had some lovely weather during the last week, almost like Summer, I don't know how long it will last but we are trying to make the most of it whilst we can. We had tea outside this evening and I generally manage to have my final snack out there before going to bed.

I had my notification for Training Camp for this year yesterday. That bit looks a little peculiar on paper but I expect that you will make sense of it. I am allocated to Plymouth (H.M.S. Raliegh) for two weeks commencing 18th Aug. It is an off shoot of Whale Island if that conveys anything to you. However it is all for a good cause and it all helps to keep my mind from wandering on to things that might have been. These Training Camps are good efforts really, you meet cadets and Officers from all parts of the country and it helps one to form an opinion as to the state of one's own unit. So far as I have been able to form an opinion, Tooting Unit is a long way from the bottom but it still has a long way to go to be 'THE' Unit. I'm not going to make excuses, though I could, for that but keep on trying to improve.

Mum has been very busy of late bottling fruit and making jam. I think that I mentioned that once before in a letter to you. She has quite a store of these now but the trouble about them is that she counts them each day so there is no chance of getting away anything. They are all stored for 'Sonny & Joey' which, as you must agree, is very poor consolation to a starving man(?). Well when you get back, I'll help you ot for I feel sure that you will only make yourselves ill trying to eat it all or will you? I see that there is another 3lb of Loganberry Jam ready for the 'Old Oak Chest' to-morrow morning.

By the way, and I don't think I have mentioned this before, Frank Gillam was married last week-end, someone, somewhere in Wales I believe. Mum met him just a few days before the catastrophy and he told her the whys & wherefores of it all. It seems only a short while ago that he helped to get our shelter dug in, these last few years have gone by quickly though at the time of passing they have seem slow.

I am improving with my typing, I can use two fingers now but I have to be careful which two. Somebody at times gets busy mixing the letters on the key board with the result that the letters come out wrong as no doubt you've noticed but I get over it. (That's my excuse and I'm stcking to it) You see what I mean, someone has pinched the 'I' just when I wanted it.

Well Old Lad, I'm afraid that this is all for this week, I see that there is not a lot of paper left. When you write to Joey give him our Love and tell him I'll try to find time to write to him personally but that we are both looking forward to having here with us and that he cannot get here too soon to suit me. Incddently I take it that you would wish me to keep these letters of his for you so I'll put them away safe in one of the draws of my desk.

Good Night Old Son, God Bless You and take care of you. We all send Love and Best Wishes including some that you do not know or rather you have not met but who are looking forward to meeting you.

Cheerio Son! Happy Landings!

Dad

Letter from Albert Taylor to Nelson Taylor. 24th June 1945. Page 3. See pages 62-65.

SOCIETY FOR THE PROTECTION OF CHILDREN

IN INDIA

Phone No. Pk. 2077.

2B, Camac Street,

Calcutta, 6th July, 1945.

1429693. Cpl. Taylor, N.D.,
7082 Servicing Echelon.,
South East Asia Command.

Dear Mr. Taylor,

Re: Joseph Miller: 6790.

I am sorry for the delay in replying to your letter in the matter of the above-named boy earlier. The letter was unfortunately mislaid by the office, and hence this delay. I was interested to hear of the developments in the case.

Having regard to the circumstances you have alluded to we sincerely trust that your endeavours to take the boy with you to England will be successful. Should, however, the case be otherwise, we shall certainly do all we can to accede to your request. We, nevertheless, feel that the Society's intervention will not be called for and that you will be able to overcome the difficulties you are at the moment confronted with.

We are glad to know that Joe is progressing favourably and shall welcome further reports from you in that regard from time to time.

With every good wish,

Yours sincerely,

GENERAL SECRETARY.

AMC/GCD.

Letter from The Society for the Protection of Children in India to Nelson Taylor. 6th July 1945. See page 67.

OFFICE OF THE DEPUTY COMMISSIONER, KHASI & JAINTIA HILLS, SHILLONG.

No. 3715/B ., Dated Shillong, the 16th July, 1945.

From

A.I. Bowman, Esqr., I.C.S.,
Deputy Commissioner, K & J Hills, Shillong,

To

The Wing Commander Snell,
7082 Servicing Echelon
C/o R.A.F. Post, Bangalore.

Subject:- No.1429693 CPL. TAYLOR.

Sir,

I have been approached by Corporal Taylor with an application for a passport for JOSEPH MILLER, a boy who is in Corporal Taylor's care. I understand that the boy was living with Corporal Taylor's unit, as 'chawalla', and was later put into an orphanage, on the instigation of the Unit Padre. As the boy was not happy there, Corporal Taylor took him out, and arranged for him to live with people in Shillong. I should be grateful if you would confirm this.

Corporal Taylor now wishes to take the boy to live with his parents in United Kingdom. As there are no papers to show that the boy has been legally adopted, the passport cannot be issued in the normal way. The boy is a British Indian subject, and in order to issue a passport, we must be satisfied that Corporal Taylor has sufficient means to maintain him, and to repatriate him, if this should be necessary. I must therefore ask for guarantees on these two heads from Corporal Taylor, and these must be approved by his Commanding Officer. I should be grateful if you would ask Corporal Taylor to furnish such guarantees on affidavit, and would send them to me with your approval.

Your obedient servant,

A. I. Bowman

Deputy Commissioner, K & J Hills,
Shillong.

/M

Letter from A. I. Bowman, Deputy Commissioner in Shillong, to Wing Commander Snell, Nelson Taylor's Wing Commander in Bangalore. 16th July 1945. Page 1. See pages 68-69.

1429693 CPL TAYLOR. N.D.

The above named airman has been responsible for the maintenance and provision of education for a young Anglo-Indian boy for some time, which has been done at the request of the airman's parents who wish to adopt the child. As his tour is nearly complete the airman wishes to make arrangements for the child to accompany him to the U.K.

His father, Mr A. H. Taylor, contacted R.A.F. Welfare in London and the attached letter is a copy of that received by him. From this it can be seen that the question is a legal one. The airman was given to understand by the Legal Adviser in Calcutta that no adoption proper as under English Law could be effected in India, but that a form of adoption could be made, making the airman the child's guardian. This the airman has ~~is willing to accept~~ effected.

The question now arises as to whether this state of guardianship is sufficient under Indian Law to allow the child to accompany the airman, as the child is too young to travel alone, being only nine years of age.

In such circumstances information is needed to ascertain to whom the passage money should be paid.

Off. for [illegible]

Letter from A. I. Bowman, Deputy Commissioner in Shillong, to Wing Commander Snell, Nelson Taylor's Wing Commander in Bangalore. 16th July 1945. Page 2. See pages 69-70.

St Mary's Church
Jamshedpur
17.8.45

Dear Mr Taylor

I am so pleased to receive so excellent an account of Joe. He appears to be quite another boy from the rascal familiar to me through Mrs Keeler. Things have speeded up since you wrote &, now you are beginning to get ready to move westwards. I don't believe that there will be delay in the occupation of the remaining territories.

Now I am about to ask you a favour. A friend priest of mine called Fr Le Tellier SJ is engaged erecting two retreat houses in Goa & has sent me these circulars hoping that I should pass them on to catholic military men desiring to have friends of theirs, now dead, remembered in the prayers of those gathering for retreats & the masses to be offered for their eternal rest beyond. You surely know some RC men or women who may desire to have friends fallen in the war remembered in this particular part of India – Goa – where St Francis Xavier began his labours & where his body is still preserved after the lapse of 4 centuries. The body is not at present in so good a condition as formerly but it is still to be seen when every

Letter from Father J. Comerford to Nelson Taylor. 17th August 1945. Page 1. See pages 70-71.

the years it is exposed.

I got a notice from the Censor department that a snapshot you mentioned in your letter was not enclosed. Perhaps you forgot it. I did receive a photo of Joly & it lies just by my ink pot. He looks quite a good little fellow, & convey to him my congratulations at his success & my hope that he will ever prove grateful to you for what you have done.

Probably Joly will never want to see India again. And I should approve. This is a country where ministers of the Gospel are needed but it's not a country where Europeans should seek careers. Australia & New Zealand are underpopulated & these places have a European population & can support many more.

I am greatly afraid that Communism is going to spread in the world & its class hatred & its godlessness are not going to heal the wounds of Society. Its leaning over towards a better condition for the workman is agreed to by all good men. Unemployment is a stain upon a nation. Every man has a right to live, to lead a life in accord with his nature – to rear a family & to have the means of support sure. Industries unfortunately don't give this security & I fear are not going to disburse in the future years. The normal life for a man is to possess land & to be able to produce & to sell his surplus. The world is topsy turvy. Yours sincerely

J Comerford 80

Letter from Father J. Comerford to Nelson Taylor. 17th August 1945. Page 2. See pages 70-71.

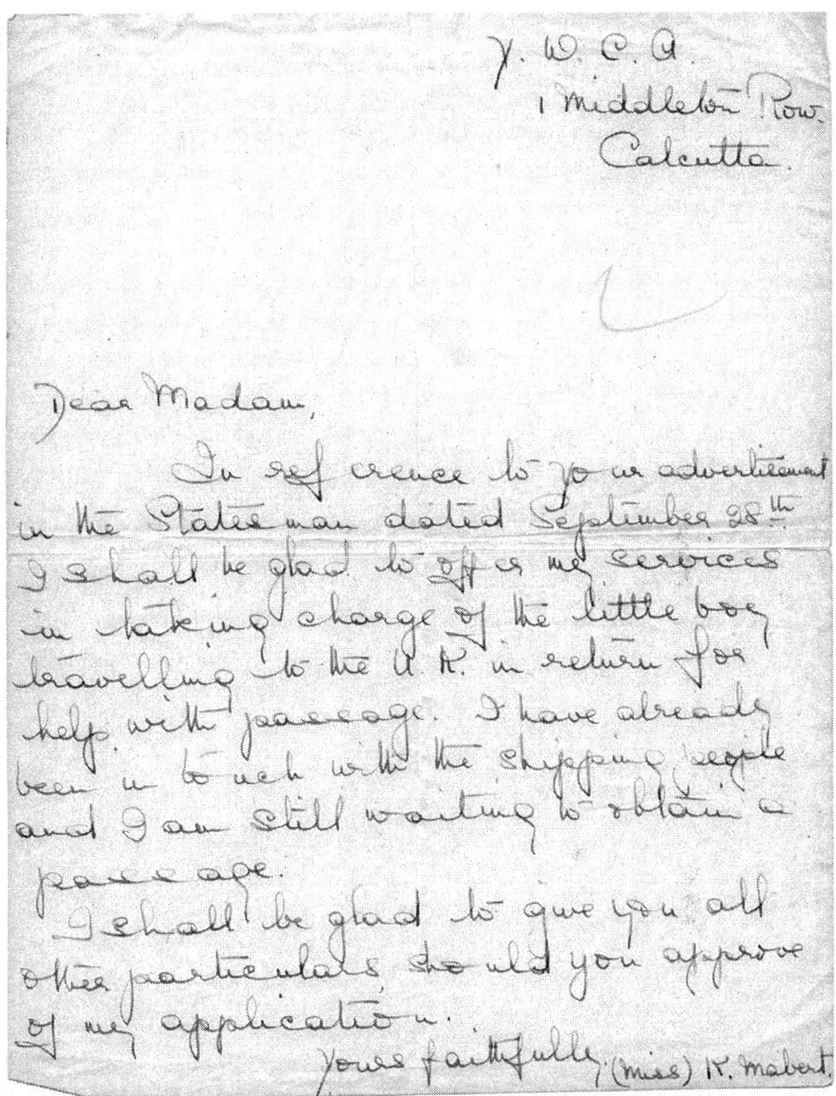

Y. W. C. A.
1 Middleton Row.
Calcutta.

Dear Madam,

In reference to your advertisement in the Statesman dated September 28th. I shall be glad to offer my services in taking charge of the little boy travelling to the U.K. in return for help with passage. I have already been in touch with the shipping people and I am still waiting to obtain a passage.

I shall be glad to give you all other particulars, should you approve of my application.

Yours faithfully, (Miss) K. Mabert.

Letter from Miss Kathleen Mabert to Nelson Taylor. 28th September 1945.

See page 72.

1429693 Cpl Taylor, N. D.
7082 Servicing Echelon,
c/o R. A. F. Post,
Bangalore.

11th Oct. 1945.

Dear Madam,

I have received your reply to my advertisment in the Personall Column of the Calcutta "Statesman". I shall be glad to let you know the further particulars you require.

I am a conscripted airman serving a tour of duty in this country which tour is now all but completed. During my travels I adopted as my ward a little orphan child to whom I am now the sole guardian and support. Since I am to return Home at any time I want to make arrangements for my child to return also. Service regulations do not appear to permit my child to travel with me, therefore I am forced to make private arrangements.

The child is Eurasian by birth, and Anglo-Indian to be precise. You had better know this now as I feel it may influence your decision. He is however, pale skinned and speaks and behaves like any ordinary kiddy. He is living with an English family in Shillong, Assam, who are friends of mine. I can assure you that this littl fellow is well worth any trouble expendedupon him.

Letter from Nelson Taylor to Miss Kathleen Mabert. 11th October 1945. Page 1. See pages 73-76.

2.

I feel that a lady would be more suitable for the position of escort to the little chap, as he has a great deal of respect for the feelings of women. He is more or less capable of looking after himself in little ways so that all the escort would need to do during the voyage would be to see that he does not fall over the rail and takes time off from playing to go to his meals.

I am prepared to pay the cost of the full fare (£70) of his escort providing she will carry out the following:

1. That she will make an application to the Civil Controller of Passages for passages for herself and the child naming herself as the child's guardian during the voyage. When I made an applicationg for a priority for him the authorities demanded the name of his escort. I was therefore, unable to make those arrangements. His priority should be in Group B no 6. which I am told is a pretty reasonable priority.

2. I want the escort to make the necessary arrangements with the Travel Agency for tickets ect. Here again, I shall not be in the country so I should find it well nigh impossible to make the arraggements myself.

Letter from Nelson Taylor to Miss Kathleen Mabert. 11th October 1945. Page 2. See pages 73-76.

3.

3. I must have the assurance of some rendezvous with the escort in the U. K. so that I can collect my little ward as quickly as possible after he arrives in the country. I live in London, but I do not expect the escort to deliver him to my home, more especially, of course, if she lives in the North. I would leave the rendezvous to the convenience of the escort, perhaps her own home might be best?

Isee by your letter that you have been a missionary in China. I had better tell you then that my little ward is a Roman Catholic. If that is not your own denomination and we decide upon an agreement, I must ask you not to attempt to interfere with the little chap's ideas, for I don't want his mind filled withjumbled ideas resulting in hisnot knowing what to believe! I expect you see my point, even though I may not have made it very clear!

The proposed date of sailing I would leave to you, the earlier the better of course. Also, I shall pay all passage money for the escort and child in advance. Any further expenses incurred by the child would be reimbursed upon the arrival in the U. K.

The child's passport is in order and arrangements for his reception at home are almost complete. It simply

Letter from Nelson Taylor to Miss Kathleen Mabert. 11th October 1945. Page 3. See pages 73-76.

4.

remains for some suitable lady to take him home for me at her own convenience. I do not anticipate any trouble from the little chap by way of behaviour, he is primarily a Boy and acts like all boys. I expect he will be sea-sick like everybody else, although he has travelled by air and not been air-sick which is much the same. This will be his first sea trip for all time.

There is one very major snag that I can see and that occurs when you are finally called for the boat. The child lives in Shillong, as I said before and it will take time to get him to you. I am told that only 10 days notice of sailing is given so that every moment would count in getting to the docks. To overcome this would you be prepared to have the child come to you some short time before you think you are due to leave, and then youcould get away on time? I think I can arrange to have him delivered to you. I can see very obvious snags to this but I cannot see the obvious way out.

If my proposals are of interest to you I would be extremely obliged by an immediate reply as time is getting short and I want to fix this thing up before I leave the country. Trusting you will give this your consideration, I remain,

Yours truly,

N. D. Taylor

Letter from Nelson Taylor to Miss Kathleen Mabert. 11th October 1945.

Page 4. See pages 73-76.

Y.W.C.A.
1 Middleton Row
Calcutta
Oct 17th 45

Dear Mr Taylor,

I am in receipt of your letter of the 11th instant regarding the care of your ward you desire accompanied to the U.K. and have noted the principal points contained therein.

I am approaching the Authorities through Messrs. Cox + Kings (Agents) Ltd Calcutta, who are my agents, for an early sea passage for myself as escort to your ward.

I regret that as I am living in a Y.W.C.A. it will not be possible to have your ward with me but some

Letter from Miss Kathleen Mabert to Nelson Taylor. 17th October 1945. Page 1. See page 76-77.

very reliable friends of mine have agreed to accommodate him at a charge of Rs 5/- per day if under 10 years of age and Rs 7/ per day if over.
In the meantime would you please see that the boy is in possession of an up to date Passport, vaccination and innoculation for Cholera certificate.
With regard to a meeting place on arrival in Britain, I shall cable you as soon as I know the date and port we shall disembark at, and it would facilitate matters if you could arrange to meet either the Steamer or the train by which we shall be travelling.
It would be advisable if you kept in touch with Messrs. Cox + Kings (Agents) Ltd. Kings House, 10 Haymarket

Letter from Miss Kathleen Mabert to Nelson Taylor. 17th October 1945. Page 2. See page 76-77.

London, S.W.1. who will be fully
informed of my movements.
I note your remarks in regard
to funds for payment of our
passages etc. and would advise
you that the money may be paid
either to my Bankers - Lloyds Bank
Ltd, 37 Chowringhee, Calcutta or
Cox & Kings (Agents) Ltd,
5 Bankshall Street, Calcutta.
I would like to add that I am a
music mistress by profession
and have had ample experience
in dealing with children. You can
rest assured that your ward will
receive every care and attention.
Yours truly, P.T.O.
Kathleen Mabert.

Letter from Miss Kathleen Mabert to Nelson Taylor. 17th October 1945. Page 3. See page 76-77.

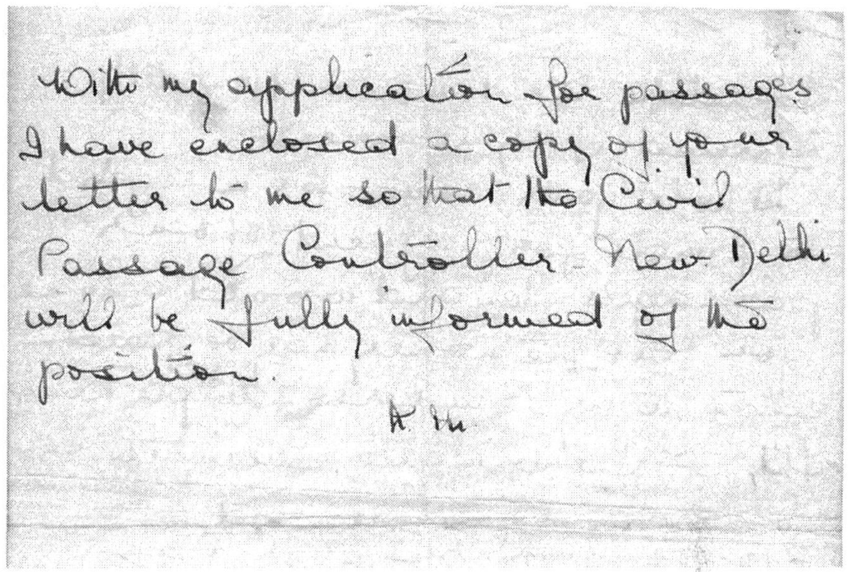

With my application for passages I have enclosed a copy of your letter to me so that the Civil Passage Controller New Delhi will be fully informed of the position.

K. M.

Letter from Miss Kathleen Mabert to Nelson Taylor. 17th October 1945. Page 4. See page 76-77.

No. M/110/PP.XI.
Government of India.
Defence Department.
New Delhi, the 31st October 1945.

To

Deputy Civil Passage Controller,
Post Box No. 1005,
BOMBAY.

Please note that the priority under Category VI-c Serial Number 33QN allotted to Miss K. Mabert has been upgraded to Category VI B Serial Number 164N. Please include Master Joseph Miller (aged 9) under this priority, as Miss Mabert has been nominated as his guardian.

for Civil Passage Controller.

Copy to:-

1. Miss K. Mabert, Y.W.C.A.
   No. 1 Middleton Row Calcutta,
   with reference to your letter dated 27.10.45.

2. 1429693 Col. Taylor N.D.
   7082, Servicing Echelon,
   c/o R.A.F. Post,
   BANGALORE.

3. Cox & Kings P.O. Box 537,
   5 Bankshall Street,
   Calcutta.

AR/REB.

Letter from Deputy Civil Passage Controller, Bombay, to Miss Kathleen Mabert. 31st October 1945. See page 80.

THE HILLBROOK SECONDARY SCHOOL FOR BOYS
HILLBROOK ROAD, S.W.17

REPORT FOR Summer Term 1947

Name Joseph Miller Age 11yrs 10mths Average Age 12yrs 5mths

Subject				Remarks
SCRIPTURE		C	T.L.W.	
ENGLISH	Composition	D	C.J.A.	Improving
	Spelling	C		
	Reading	D		
FOREIGN LANGUAGES	French	C+	D.M.	Keen.
MATHEMATICS		D.	T.L.W.	
	Geometry	C	[illegible]	
HISTORY		E	C.J.A.	
GEOGRAPHY		C	C.A.P.	
SCIENCE		B	T.L.W.	
ART		B-	C.A.P.	
CRAFTS	Woodwork	A	[illegible]	
OTHER SUBJECTS				

Conduct Good Attendance Satisfactory

GENERAL REPORT—
Joseph is very keen but at times [illegible] ... the ... [illegible]

Master

Parent C. F. Gooding Head Master

1000 (F9508.24) 16.8.46

Report card from Hillbrook Secondary School for Boys. Summer 1947. See page 102.

London County Council

THE HILLBROOK SECONDARY SCHOOL FOR BOYS

HILLBROOK ROAD, S.W.17

REPORT FOR Ex 1948-49

Name Joseph Miller Age 14 Average Age 14 3/12

Subject		Exam	Effort	Remarks	
SCRIPTURE		B	B		
ENGLISH	Composition	C	B	Is making steady progress	J.C.
	Formal	C	B		
FOREIGN LANGUAGES					
MATHEMATICS		D	B	Has tried hard	JSC
HISTORY		C	B	A good worker	N.J.
GEOGRAPHY		C	A.	A good year's work	JB
SCIENCE		D	B	Term work good	[illegible]
Biology		C	C	average	[illegible]
ART		C	B	Has done some good work	JSC
CRAFTS	Woodwork	A	A	A good years work	[illegible]
	Geometry	E	B	Good work throughout the year.	[illegible]
OTHER SUBJECTS	MUSIC	—	B		N.J.

Conduct Ex Attendance Ex

GENERAL REPORT— He has done a good years work. He works conscientiously and has made considerable progress. Takes an active interest in all the school activities.

J S Clifton Master

Parent

C.A. Gosling Head Master

1000 (F9509.24) 10.5.46

Report card from Hillbrook Secondary School for Boys. Summer 1948. See pages 109-110.

FOR BOYS.
School UPPER TOOTING, S.W.17.

REPORT OF PROGRESS July 1950 Date

Name Miller Joseph　　Number in class 28

Class Technical (Upper)　　Position in class

		Initials of master mistress	Remarks
Scripture	Satisfactory	LED	
English Spelling	C-	LED	Works well & tries hard.
Grammar	C-	LED	
Composition	C	LED	
History	B	NJ	
Geography	C+	JB	
Science	B	EB	Good work
Biology	B	JWS	
Art	A-	JB	An extremely hard worker; has done some excellent work.
Craft Metalwork	A-	EJE	Keen & careful worker.
Needlework			
Arithmetic & Algebra	C	LED	
Domestic Science			
Handicraft Wood	A-	HM	A good worker.
Other Subjects: Machine Drawing	B.	VJB	Very good work done
Conduct	Satisfactory	LED	
Attendance	Satisfactory	LED	

Class Master L. E. Darrington
~~Class Mistress~~

Head Master W. A. Amadge
Head Mistress

Parent

200,000—(Q.12836-21)—3.3.39—7148

Report card from Hillbrook Secondary School for Boys. July 1950. See page 117.

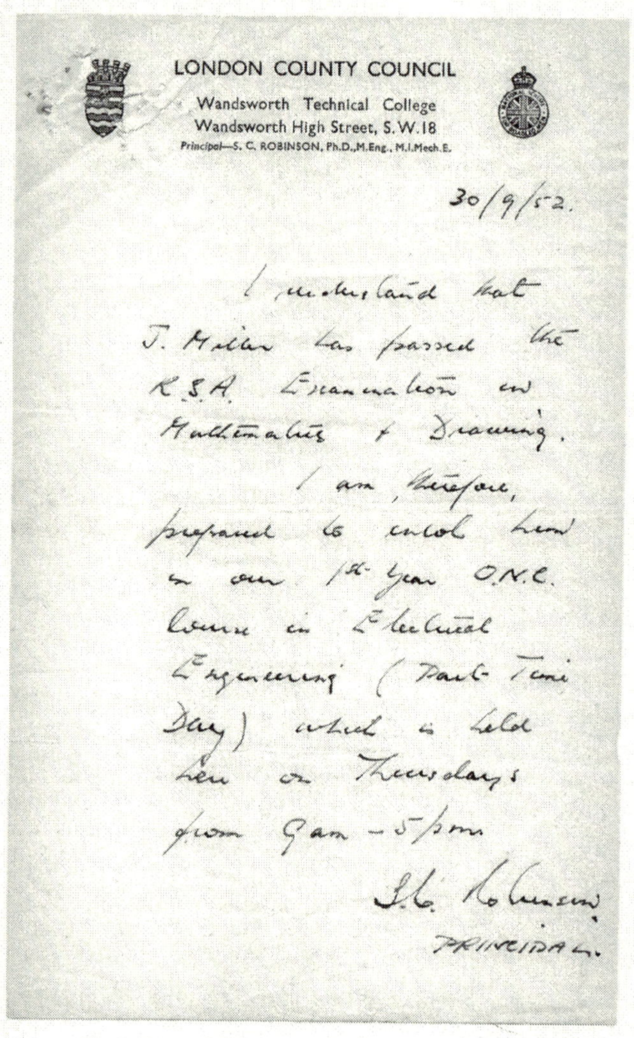

LONDON COUNTY COUNCIL
Wandsworth Technical College
Wandsworth High Street, S.W.18
Principal—S. C. ROBINSON, Ph.D., M.Eng., M.I.Mech.E.

30/9/52.

I understand that J. Miller has passed the R.S.A. Examination in Mathematics & Drawing.

I am, therefore, prepared to enrol him in our 1st Year O.N.C. Course in Electrical Engineering (Part-Time Day) which is held here on Thursdays from 9am – 5pm

S.C. Robinson
PRINCIPAL.

Letter dated 30th September 1952 from the Wandsworth Technical College to the London Electricity Board about my performance at school. The report reads, "I maintain that J. Miller has passed the R.S.A. Examination on Mathematics and Drawing. I am therefore prepared to enroll him in our 1st year O.N.C. course in Electrical Engineering (Part-Time Day) which is held here on Thursdays from 9am–5pm." See page 129.

ROYAL SOCIETY FOR THE ENCOURAGEMENT
OF ARTS, MANUFACTURES AND COMMERCE
LONDON

Founded in 1754 Incorporated in 1847

TECHNICAL GROUPED
COURSE EXAMINATION IN ELEMENTARY SUBJECTS

Joseph Miller

a candidate of the London County Council, sat, in the year 1952, for the Examination prescribed by the Royal Society of Arts, and though not successful in the requisite subjects for the award of the Grouped Certificate has passed in the undermentioned subjects:—

Mathematics
Technical Drawing

Secretary of the Royal Society of Arts

Certificate from the Royal Society for the Encouragement of Arts, Manufactures and Commerce London. As mentioned in the above letter from Wandsworth Technical College, this certificate states that while I did not pass the Grouped Course Examination in Elementary Subjects, I did pass the exams for Mathematics and Technical Drawing. See page 129.

Principal
LESLIE E. PEAD

LONDON COUNTY COUNCIL
Upper Tooting Junior Commercial
and Junior Technical Evening Institute
Fircroft Road School
Upper Tooting, S.W.17

Telephone
BALham 5311

1/10/52

The Southern Sub-area Manager
L.E.B.

Dear Sir

Joseph Miller has attended the above institute for about 2 years. (in the Technical classes). He was regular and punctual, and of good discipline. A report on his work and progress will be prepared after consultation with the various instructors, and should be ready within a few days.

E. Crops
(Deputy Principal)

Letter dated 1st October 1952 about my performance at school, sent from the Upper Tooting Junior Commercial and Junior Technical Evening Institute to the Southern Sub-Area Manager at the London Electricity Board. The report reads, "Dear Sir, Joseph Miller has attended the above institute for about 2 years (in the Technical Classes). He was regular and punctual, and of good discipline. A report on his work and progress will be prepared after consultation with the various institutions, and should be ready within a few days." See page 129.

London County Council

Form T4/206
(Technical)

EVENING INSTITUTES—TERM REPORT

UPPER TOOTING J. C. & J. T. EVENING INSTITUTE,
FIRCROFT ROAD, TOOTING, S.W.17.

Report for ~~term~~ Year ended July 1952

Name MILLER Joseph Course Technical

Subject	Attendance Actual	Attendance Possible	Progress	Initials of Instructor
English	35	35	Excellent progress. A good worker. Always does his best.	S.M.
Mathematics	35	35	Very good progress, shows a keen interest in this subject.	S.M.
Science				
Technical Drawing	68	68	Attendance very good. Progress excellent. Shows a keen interest in Drg.	W.V.J.
Workshop Practice	70	70	Attendance excellent, showed keen interest in the work and made good progress.	A.B.

GENERAL REMARKS— Royal Society of Arts Technical Examinations Stage 1; passed in Mathematics and Technical Drawing.

The next term begins

Leslie G. Read
Principal of Institute.

3000 (F7931-3) 2.9. 4

Report card from the Upper Tooting Junior Commercial and Junior Technical Evening Institute. July 1952. See page 131.

LIST OF ILLUSTRATIONS

ABOUT THE AUTHOR

Joe Miller has lived a life of adventure. Against all odds, he survived as a homeless orphan in India during World War II until a fortuitous encounter with a British serviceman gave him a second chance at life. His personal philosophy is to always get back up, no matter how many times you get knocked down. He now lives in Medicine Hat, Canada, with his wife, Beryl. His children and grandchildren also reside in Canada. *Who Am I* is his first book.

Made in the USA
Middletown, DE
23 May 2021

39455049R00135